Antonette,

thank you.

Hidden
Senses

love

15/6/23

Ann Traynor

Crann Draíochtúil

Published by: Crann Draíochtúil

Copyright © 2023 Ann Traynor

Cover Design by Cathal O' Gara
Interior Layout Design by Sandeep Likhar

ISBN: 9798844184956

Table of Contents

Dedications

For my children: Ally-Ann, Jodie and Jessica
My Sun. My Moon. My star.

I know how challenging life can get and how the unfolding of situations and circumstances can prove to be very difficult to navigate.

You are amazing and have unique, remarkable gifts to share. I'm eternally grateful you chose me to guide you through this lifetime as your mum. My role is so simple: to hold you up when you fall down, feed you when you're hungry, change your nappy when you stank, give you tissues when your nose dripped, wipe your tears when you cry, hug you when you need holding, stand by you when you need strength; and empower each of you with the knowledge of life – that your destiny awaits. The easiest part of my role with you is the unconditional love.

Do what you love, laugh as much as you can. Try never to have regrets; they hold us back. There are lessons to be learnt, mistakes will be made.

Whatever the dream, go for it. Dream Big!

This book is my insight, my wisdom and the knowledge that I've picked up on my journey along life's path.

My words will always be for the greater and higher good, for all to find them when the time is right. A healing thread is woven into every word written.

You each are my higher and greater good. This little book of me is for you to always believe in the magic.

You are made up of stardust. All the planets perfectly aligned for us to be together – we will have many lifetimes together to get it right. After every fall you will rise back up and will understand more.

> *Out there somewhere there is a love who will never dream*
> *of calling you too much. Who speaks like you, in poetry,*
> *candlewax and stardust. Who runs outside on stormy nights to*
> *howl at the moon. Who collects bones and sings incantations*
> *and talks to the ancestors. And that lover, when you find him or*
> *her, will see and know you – just as you are and just as you*
> *should be. And, they will say yes. Yes, you. I will go there with*
> *you. I have been waiting for this –*
> **Jeanette Le Blanc**

Mark

Thank you for all you do and for being you. You brought me the most significant of lessons: what love can do and be. We can't have the beauty of the rose without its thorns.

I will always choose you.

We've travelled so many lifetimes – and for whatever sorcery brought us together, I will be eternally grateful. If it weren't for you, I wouldn't have found my purpose and light that I see every single day through our girls. You're a great Dad and we all love you.

Thank You. Thank You. Thank You.

For Michelle

I would like to make a special dedication to my friend, my confidante, Michelle. The journey you face is a turbulent one. I will walk by your side as you always did for me.
You've always brought so much light into my world, my friend.
I love you.

Preface

I wish to express my sincere gratitude to you, the reader, for taking an interest in my way of being and my thought process. This makes you part of my journey to enlightenment.

Wherever you are in life, there is always room for improvement and growth.

Life is the longest journey you will take, the roads less travelled are the roads you should walk, enlightening people along the way with your light.

Doing the sacred internal work outlined in *Hidden Senses* will allow you to progress along these roads, organically and naturally – we cannot force our way or control the system. You will learn to practise being present with your self through your thoughts, feelings and instincts. Our body remembers everything, so this kind of constant cleanse will bring you into a space of clarity.

It's only when we are in the dark that we find our light and reach our potential.

By helping others through their transitions, and by listening, you will learn that we are all very similar and have shared experiences that we can help each other through.

Your inner compass and guide has led you here today to reading these words. My intention is for your spiritual growth and wellbeing to flourish and transcend any energetic boundaries and walls you may feel trapped by.

Love is the undercurrent we all are familiar with – it's what brings us together yet can keep us apart. The great divide causes so much heartache, but by leaning into the whys that are connected to your story, you can begin to take baby steps into the unknown.

With new knowledge you can take action and feel your way through everyone and everything that life has to throw at you. A new way of Being opens you up for new possibilities, doorways into your temple will swing open for you to breathe in new cleansed air.

This is when your story of healing begins.
It's like any other story, it has to write itself.

You get to marinate in and absorb the energy that you are, with the energy you are surrounded by, learning to lean into what feels familiar to you in your now – what's yours, what's not. Practising this allows you to understand the subtle differences that may be taking place around you. Learning to name the emotion you feel and why it's there, asking why it has revisited you. Taking whatever time you need to process it is entirely up to you. The deeper the wound, the longer the process.

When you are ready, you will find yourself on the other side of all that unease and uncomfortableness, finding your true self once again, to rebuild and regain your strength and confidence. The time will come when you are ready to surrender. Surrendering with love is the easiest and only way through it.

This can bring great change, enhancing your life by helping you to understand yourself through the ups the downs; your internal ebb and flow. Clearing new pathways for you to Pave the Way.

Not all storms come to disrupt your life,
Some come to clear your path.
Anonymous

Thank You. Thank You. Thank You for your purchase. Get comfortable, snuggle up and let me take your mind into another dimension which connects us all to the spiritual realms that we all can learn from.

I am a 13th-generation Reiki Master Teacher for the lineage of Shiki Ryoho Usui, Dublin, Ireland.

I hold workshops for teaching Reiki Self-Healing Level 1, 2 and 3 alongside holding Reiki Shares.

I offer Psychic Development workshops and by the end of 2023 I plan to teach Tarot workshops. For those interested in attending these classes, keep an eye on my social media platforms. I'm on Instagram, Facebook and Linkedin as Ann Traynor Wellness Centre. I'm also the author of *Hidden Forces*, which is the perfect complement to *Hidden Senses*.

Google Ann Traynor and you'll find me on these platforms and how to connect with me.

Website is: anntraynorwellnesscentre.ie.

With so much love from your soul sister from this and another lifetime!

Ann Traynor

Introduction

Everything is connected. It is without doubt my life's purpose to remind each of you that we are connected on a soul level. I've had too many experiences that cannot be explained as coincidences: I've heard the whispers; I have the certainty of knowing without understanding, enlightened moments of clarity that I cannot comprehend or explain; I have a way of understanding that allows me to move forward with ease (most days!); I have felt energy move around me, working alongside me; I've noticed the signs and followed every one of them, which has led me here to this moment, writing these words.

We Are Energy

Within the pages of words in this little book of me, I would like for you to recognise yourself as an energetic being. As you read, take what resonates with you, and the rest – just let it go.

My healing journey began to take shape in the form of Reiki in 2018, therefore I will honour its code of conduct, and take you through the pathway to understanding that I chose to walk myself, with guidance from my Reiki Ascended Masters. I know they can also guide you towards your potential as they did me.

To understand the spiritual concepts of Reiki healing even more, I reluctantly became a teacher to further enhance my knowledge of healing and how it worked. You see, I was the biggest sceptic – which I feel makes it even more special for me. I had no choice but to dive deeply into trusting its powers.

I was completely lost, hurting, disempowered and disabled from living a healthy enjoyable life. My thought processes had become completely negative. I trusted no one. I assumed everybody had an angle and wanted something from me. I was paranoid beyond comprehension, pushing everybody away from me, unable to heal the pain and hurt I was feeling. I felt the whole world was against me and nothing seemed to go as planned.

You see, I was always a planner; it's part of my blueprint. It's a gift that threw me into a learning abyss called *You Can't Plan or Control Everything* – huge, mammoth lesson for me.

"The Universe has a plan for you."

I have come to understand this concept, after long deliberation with my self.

I was everybody else's personal organiser, I was great for making plans, organising the events. I was a natural, therefore: "Ann would sort that out, she's good at that type of stuff". Pass the buck to Ann – and I was happy to help anybody out, especially if it was for the greater good, I was all over it. I felt fulfilled, finishing and ticking off anything I believed was an achievement and success. I was and am still great at rallying the troops, getting everybody involved, building the energy – keeping it going.

I felt I was the glue that kept friendships together, the phone calls, the nights out, booking the restaurants, maybe even picking people up along the way. I was the "go to" person who would sort it out.

However, when it came to my own personal life, I felt I wasn't in control. Life had placed me in quarantine long before covid – I had a series of unfortunate events that took their toll, leaving me with an overall feeling of being separated, lonely and disconnected.

The Universe had once again decided my fate, forcing me into a dark corner where I had zero understanding of what was going on. I convinced myself along the way that it was just me.

There was something wrong, though I couldn't quite put my finger on it. Changes needed to be made in order for me to fill the void of emptiness I was feeling. It was just this constant void that came over me; day after day, it took form outside of me and then grew into something much bigger.

I can't articulate it very well in words: it's a feeling, a blanket of nothingness, a breeze of non-existence that swept through me. One minute I was feeling everything going at a snail's pace, the next I was catapulted forward. The space in between all that was "the void".

No matter how much I tried to fill this void, it just made me unhappier. I would repeat the cycle every day, searching for what fulfilment felt like, washing my floors away as if I was going to find it there somehow, cleaning the house, washing clothes, ironing clothes, endless days of mundane conversations of checking in on how everybody else was doing.

I never really stopped to see how I was doing. After all, I knew myself best (I thought).

There was no doubt about it, I was struggling. When I recognised this, the conversations within my mind started to shift. I had an urgency in me to fix it, fix me. Come up with a plan, Ann! You're good at this, this is where you shine.

Everybody else seemed to think I was more than capable – but the truth was, I didn't feel like I could make a plan. Little me once again feeling torn and separated from everything that kept me together. Something deep within was telling me I couldn't do it. The voice I heard from within came from a place I recognised as fear. My body trembled and I fell down like a tonne of bricks.

I had been there before – my body felt carried by a raging torrent. Was I going to be swept away altogether?

A voice came and echoed through me, a calmer voice, softer. Saying: "No, you're not going to be swept away. We are going to do this together, step-by-step. Take each day as it arrives and make some changes that will help you and others along the way. We will direct you back to love. It's not going to be easy. We will take you onto a path of remembrance where you will heal on a soul level and release all that doesn't serve you."

To be honest, I had a lot of releasing to do, but my reaction to that came in the form of resistance. The resistance of releasing was so great I couldn't ignore it. But I made a commitment that day to myself, to show up. This was alien to me. I had never done anything like it before. It's so much easier helping other people, but this was definitely an inside job: I had to help myself. Literally. Just like escaping a jail sentence I had imposed upon my own mind.

Focussing Attention
So here I am, being directed back to love through self in order to help you. Yes, you, who have found my little book of words that are laced with insight, wisdom and knowledge of the cosmos and earth magic.

This was the first plan and I had no control over it. I fully surrendered and put my trust in an energy I couldn't see or make sense of. That was also when I knew I was unlocking doors into a part of *me*, a place of complete darkness that I had to revisit and heal. Heightened Hidden Senses came into play, offering me moments of clarity that would reach me in the depths of my loss and despair.

My trust grew and my story began to reveal itself to me through meditation. Focusing my attention on nothing heightened my awareness to everyone and everything connected to me. By reading and studying I enlightened myself about my energetic body and started my healing journey into the unknown – into the darkness with my eyes wide shut, learning to feel my way around any emotional, energetic scars that remained within me or on my physical body.

I am going to take you deeper into what I have come to learn about our "Hidden Senses".

I want to teach you how to tap into them. Become the observer, gather your own information – sit in meditation and watch life unfold for you like a beautiful movie that was already written for you to remind you and bring you back to where you came from – which is love.

You are the love story that unfolded out into this world. You are part of my Love Story.

Ann

Hidden Senses

Reiki opened a door in my mind and gave me the tools to work with to invoke change within my self. Now I can take you with me into my own further development, which is a deeper self-awareness that opens even more channels and doorways within the mind.

This enables me to feel beyond what the eyes can see – it's the space outside of the physical that is of interest to me now. This allows me a wider perspective. What you see, hear, smell or touch may not be all it seems.

Let's take it up a notch by learning about your intuition and how it evolves with you along your journey of enlightenment. Let me explain what it may feel like for you, too.

Get your highlighter ready and take what you can from my words.

Energy Matters

Every day comes with new experiences that bring us different energies – from the surface, every-day energies of minor upheavals that unexpectedly change our plans, to major life events that have a huge rippling effect throughout our whole system. These can change our lives. We are all conditioned differently to how we react and respond to situations and adverse circumstances.

For example, adapting to a new way of being can be difficult if we lose somebody who played a significant role in our life, someone who validated our existence like no other. We all have that person, or people, who helped us navigate the world through understanding our self. They made life look so easy. They always managed to have that familiar smile, that welcoming hug that made us feel safe, secure and allowed us to feel love with no boundaries: a space where there is only unconditional love, truth, trust and a strong sense of belonging.

We seek this from the moment we feel or sense it has been taken from us. If we lose someone we love, we feel abandoned, alone and separated from a love that once kept us strong and connected.

These life-changing experiences of loss never leave us; they always remain within us. So does what we felt – and still feel – for the person we loved and lost. When you go through this kind of loss, remember: everything is energy. The energy of the person you love makes you an embodiment of them that remains here. Like your heartbeats, they are still with you – love vibrational energy never dies.

You are manifested into human form. Every organ, cell, tissue, fibre, flesh, blood, bones, skin – everything that keeps you together, that makes you into the human being you are – including your energy – goes way beyond your physical existence, through invisible layers in the ether, and makes up your auric field.

When we break through the walls and boundaries of our physical layer and step into our feelings, we open our selves to feel every emotion that our pain body felt. We can begin to heal our tired wounded self that caused some road blocks along our pathways of understanding, and we can begin to tap into everything beyond our physical walls, understanding that we are all woven into the same fabric that is as old as time, and are connected on a soul level.

We have this memory chip in our minds that holds all our information, maybe memories long forgotten, but your body remembers everything. Your body is designed to send you signals, such as your intuition. The Universe's job is to send you reminders /

messages in the form of signs and symbols along the way. You need to be open to receive the messages and, most importantly, to trust what you are getting. We tend to brush off such messages, signs and symbols, thinking we are "imagining" them.

It's up to you how much you desire to know, how much you want to delve into each experience that will take you into an understanding of your life, its meaning and purpose.

We are forever in a constant flow through many layers of understanding. Any thoughts you may have, acknowledge them – say thank you and let them go.

We have every-day surface thoughts that can take you from one space of doing into another, or those which can cause minor interferences along the way.

We also have a train of thoughts full of shared memories that can go much deeper into the abyss of self, that may cause major distractions and disturbances within your whole system. Journalling is a fantastic tool that can keep you present with your thoughts and feelings, in the here and now, allowing you to become an observer as you blend conflicting internal forces into your blank pages. Writing allows you to go deeper into understanding why a particular experience visited you and why you decided to take the train in the first place!

Chakras

Our chakras are an important part of our spiritual and psychic development; they work with the natural energies of the Universe. For a more in-depth view into each chakra, please refer to my *Hidden Forces* book, where you can explore yourself a little deeper. Knowledge of your chakras can be very helpful in working through any blockages and barriers which we all face as we travel along the path of change and transformation into enlightenment.

The chakras draw in any energy they encounter on a vibratory level – good as well as bad. They regulate the flow of energy throughout your whole system, based on the decisions you have made and the conditioning within your life.

They are not physical but are aspects of our consciousness. They correspond to different times in our lives, from childhood to old age. We learn through difficult experiences and these lessons heighten our awareness of others. Carrying the vibration of our experiences is part of who we are in the now. These experiences will remain within our energetic field, until we choose to turn them into a wake-up call for our healing to commence. This, in turn, directs us on to a spiritual path taking centre stage within our heart space and opens us up to receiving love.

Negative energy can find its way into our chakras, resulting in blockages and barriers, which is why we should clear and cleanse them regularly.

Becoming familiar with your chakras is a great start to opening yourself up to your intuition – that still, small voice within which echoes generations of whispers from the Divine, Higher Self, God, The Universe, Guardian Angels, Ascended Masters, Spirit Guides…whatever that higher power is for you that is outside of you, that works through you when you need and seek guidance.

Intuition can often be signposts – messengers – that were shown or sent to you, and perhaps went unnoticed or you discounted them as "just" coincidences. But remember – if you were "listening", your body responded and it stopped you in that moment.

Your physical senses nudged you, maybe you saw something that seemed odd or out of place, smelled a rat, a conversation left a sour taste in your mouth or maybe you heard inner guidance from a space deep within you. Overall, you felt it and it travelled through you, sending a rippling effect through your existence and may have even brought you into a space of confusion. Your intuition kicked in at that moment and either you listened to it, or maybe life got in the way or you just didn't recognise it.

When you feel something is different but can't quite put your finger on why, this is your intuition talking and communicating with you. You may have decided to brush it off, but a question would have surfaced within you, a question that will revisit you through conversations you hear from other people. Your Guides will send messengers that are carrying information to you. People from your soul family, who were always meant to cross your path, will meet you at life's crossroads and roundabouts. Your intuition may have tried to get your attention by raising a question in your mind, but was met with a diversion of "it's probably just my imagination". You may have chosen to ignore or brush off the coincidence as a silly concept or notion.

Next time this happens, listen to the voice inside you. Pay attention to it, what it feels like, sounds like – and what you feel when it nudges you. Learn to recognise it as valid and not just "all in my mind" or "just my imagination". Soon, whenever your intuition ignites, you will recognise it and will find it easier to act on.

Good Vibrations

Negative thoughts can lower your chakras' vibratory level. When you notice negative thoughts creeping in, anything that may bring you into a space of self-sabotage, feeling the wobble and spiralling sensation taking hold, focus on expressing these feelings through what your intuition guides you towards, whether it be through movement, sound or stillness – anything that will provide you with growth, enhancing your life skills in a more positive way, enlightening you.

Our body is a powerful tool and is constantly gathering information. Our chakras are aligned along our spine – they also gather and soak up information and feelings, and deposit these into our organs and glands. Different organs and glands are associated with a particular chakra, depending on the location within your body. For example, the adrenal gland is connected to our root chakra. When our fight-or-flight response is triggered, our stress is heightened, adrenalin is released, and we experience fear. Fear being the main (negative) culprit demon of the root chakra. The less fear we hold in our body, the more relaxed and at ease we will be – and vice versa.

When we focus on harnessing good positive experiences, this offers a more pleasant and / or peaceful loving way for us to look at situations. That, in turn, invokes calmness within the whole body, thereby creating new experiences which seek out a higher frequency and resonance with life. The Universe works with your vibrational frequency. So, if you are in a constant state of fear, you are manifesting more fear.

So, what's the life you want to have? The Universe works with you, not against you. When you trust and believe in yourself and what you're capable of, the Universe will work with you, too.

I believe that our chakras are different levels of consciousness When they are functioning efficiently, you will hold a greater and broader psychic awareness. Whilst doing any practices to enhance your psychic awareness and development, it's really good to do a chakra opening / cleansing ritual beforehand.

To open and cleanse your chakras, guided meditations can work best. Begin the process of visualisation by opening your mind, a little more every time, and envisage white light. Work with the white light and envisage it entering you, coming down through your crown chakra, and pushing any negative thoughts and energy down and out through your feet, back into the earth.

Place your hands together palm-to-palm with the intention that you are about to cleanse and clear your whole chakra system. Rub your palms together slightly then separate your palms and feel the life force energy flowing from one to the other.

Then simply place your hands on each chakra in turn, bringing your awareness into these areas of your body while amplifying the white light energy into each space. Acknowledge your presence in the now, notice how your body responds and how you feel in these moments of silence with yourself. Notice if you feel any tension held within your body. Make a mental note of what chakra it is connected to – that will give you a clue to what inner work you have to do.

Awakening Intuition

The spiritual field can be confusing. The new story you create to enhance your gifts is one of integration and collaboration with your creative self.

Intuition is a gift and a super power that we all possess – if you choose to pay attention to it. It's about trusting yourself. We are not taught how to use our intuition, although some people definitely have the advantage of having more access to it. Being female naturally enhances it and it evolves through how we creatively express it. It's also something that may be in your family bloodline, through your ancestry.

There are lots of tools you can use that enhance your intuition, which in turn allows your psychic abilities to flourish. The Universe is co-creating with you via the Laws of Attraction, where everything is determined – everything that comes into your life and everything that you experience. Through the magnetic power of your thoughts, like attracts like.

What you think about, you bring about.

Your thoughts are the internal light switch that turns you from Off to On, taking you from darkness into light, from the depths of heartache and loss to light and love laced with understanding.

Awareness of the power of our thoughts and intuition is what I like to call our "Awakening". Such awareness begins the process of freeing ourselves from layers of conditioning of how we perceive energy, and our initial response or reaction to the situations we find ourselves in.

Situations that I believe have been placed in front of us like a fog through which we have to learn to navigate with our thoughts, feelings, emotions and behaviour. Basically, it feels like being blindfolded and having to trust that the best outcome will allow us to be seen, to feel loved, safe and secure as we continually soul search for the love that we came from in the first place. Remember, desire runs deep: hold the desire within you to feel special and loved.

Expressing yourself in your true form will get you to the other side of the fog. There are dark clouds that hover over us all from time to time, activating internal storms laced with fear. We all have fear, too. Access your fears and you will open doorways within you that will jolt you into new possibilities, turning crises into opportunities for your growth and understanding.

People will cross your path offering deep reminders of who you are, and who you are not. We are all extensions of each other. From childhood to adulthood, we are playing hide and seek. We seek, find and see ourselves through others.

When facing difficult times, you may hide and go within for you may be facing a shadow aspect of yourself that doesn't fit within your "now". However, I feel this is also a form of fear coming up from the depths of our souls into the light. To deal with fear and pain, we must face them within the four walls of the human container we find ourselves in.

First, find your light. This starts off as a self-commitment – sacred, internal work that starts with convincing yourself just how much worth you hold. We can lose touch with ourselves during the storms of life and mindless every-day chatter, losing ourselves in the roles and labels we have placed on ourselves and one another.

Some roles take a lot more strength, stamina, agility, trust, love and integrity to hold. We may break from time to time but we always find our way back home to love. Love is an eternal truth that we all share and connect with. You play the major role within your story and life; it all starts and ends with you. You are unique in every sense.

So, finding yourself tangled in the roots of conditioning isn't pleasant – but extracting yourself isn't difficult. Just be who you are. Trust where life is taking you. Collect those golden nuggets of happiness and understanding, and hold onto them as reminders of who you are.

Be consistent and persistent: set a goal of harnessing your power and light and guiding it back into your self; and practise this. Fragments of you that you no longer hold space for will dissipate through time, and leave you when you are ready to heal and let them go. You've got to wholeheartedly surround yourself in an energy of patience and trust. This is when you find your flow and you get to choose your channel of concentration.

Bringing dedication and determination to your strength of will and character, as well as sewing intentional seeds for what you seek, will strengthen your core beliefs, values and behaviour so you can move forward with what you hold dear. You will find or create that missing link within which connects all you are to all that is.

Clair(e) is a French word that means clear. When you clear and unblock your energy centres it invokes clarity to help you move forward. A journey of self-discovery involves you facing an internal climb of home-truths to reach the peaks of understanding your true self, warts and all, releasing any pain or discomfort from your experiences and replacing that with love. The journey back down from the mountain is equally as important. This involves you being grateful for every person you met along the way who provided you with the insight, knowledge and wisdom to get you up the mountain and back down it again.

You have to take responsibility for your own part in your own story; nobody else is responsible for your actions. When you accept responsibility for your own actions, it encourages honesty with your self.

It's so much easier for us to hold onto a grudge or negative thoughts towards others who may have caused us to feel a wide range of lower-vibrational feelings from an unpleasant situation. As I've said, our thoughts and feelings produce energy, so when we are in a negative situation we can very easily get caught up in the process of lower-vibrational feelings such as frustration, anger, fear, shame and guilt. This can have a detrimental effect, rippling through our whole being, mentally, emotionally and physically.

It's so much easier for us to blame someone else, and point the finger away from ourselves. Blaming is a huge part of the process of observing, as we do it all the time: the whole "he said / she said", where everything gets lost in translation because we all have different opinions, perspectives and stories. It is like a boomerang effect.

Learn to notice your knee-jerk reactions. This takes time, there is no easy way through it; I wish there was. Acknowledging our feelings is part of healing. Saying or doing the wrong thing at the wrong time is classic: we've all been there – and continue to go there. Where you were (or are) energetically at that (or this) time in your life may be all you have ever known. It's possible you're stuck there. Stuck at a time when your brain said one thing but your gut was screaming something else. Learn to trust your gut.

It takes time to unwind and rediscover yourself after ignoring your instincts for years. Staying stuck in the mindset of "should've", "would've", "could've", "if only..." keeps you mired in a state of regret and / or worry, which sets off a train of negative thought patterns.

The good news is – you can change. Make a pact with yourself today, to make an intentional shift in your behaviour – decide that you will listen to your gut instincts, that you will listen to your self. Decide that you will have and say all the right words when you need to. Words hold a vibration. Negative words (and thoughts) hold negative vibrations. Cutting ties from negative vibrations and energy sets you free. By doing so, you are allowing space within you to navigate yourself towards new, higher, vibrational frequencies. Positive, life-enhancing ones.

Opening Channels

We all have some psychic abilities. Every one of us has a natural intuitive ability, so I am going to offer you some insight into how to open these channels and for you to ask yourself the question – which ability are you using naturally? Which is the strongest for you?

You are here, having been pulled towards wanting to know more about this subject, which tells me you are already in the belief system that you have psychic abilities – so this is a great start!

Some of you may be highly attuned to your senses, or you may be completely unaware how to access them – but we just want to know more about them, right?

Being attuned to your psychic abilities is about being consciously aware of how your body is responding or reacting to people, places and things you are surrounded by or influenced by whilst going through your day. Not as easy as it sounds – after all, we have life throwing us all sorts of curveballs to keep us busy with forgetting, and not allowing the gifts that are genetically encoded into every one of us to flourish.

They are without doubt there, although we can lose touch with these senses and may let things slide for so long. That can form blocks around our third eye and crown chakras, affecting our conditioning and self-belief.

You may predominately feel things through one of these clairs I've mentioned – often, intuition may come in through one of your least strong clairs. It's important to be aware of these different abilities and to practise and strengthen them throughout your intuitive development. This book will help you, as will your own further study.

Each of your psychic senses is attached to your physical senses, which are integrated within each of your chakra's potential, so clearing out and healing these energy centres can have a powerful effect on your psychic abilities.

Let's start from the beginning and take it from there. I have added the relevant physical senses corresponding to each chakra, and a little insight into each one which may hold a resonance for you.

Clairalience:
Clear Sense of Smell

Root Chakra

Our sense of smell is known as the strongest evoker of memory, bringing back long-forgotten images to us.

Aromatherapy and / or incense can evoke and awaken this energy centre's potential for remembrance.

We can usually connect a fragrance to a person or memory; it never leaves us.

Our journey of self-discovery starts at our root.

This chakra is connected to the Earth element.

It deals with survival and is blocked by fear.

Located at the base of your spine, the root chakra represents your primary needs as a human being. When it is healthy, it's much easier for us to trust ourselves and go with the flow of life. If our material needs are met, our prosperity and finances flow.

This chakra offers a safe place for you to have trust.

It is fully developed by seven years of age. Our Roots. Our Family. Our Tribe.

Its energy colour is red, and its mantra / sound seed is LAM. Chanting this sound and visualising this colour helps you channel your full focus and awareness to this energy centre within your body.

This chakra represents the foundations on which we stand, from our parents, siblings, grandparents, extended family and ancestors – our whole lineage way beyond the grave; people in our bloodline that walked similar routes before us. Exploring our history and where we come from is a rabbit hole that all earth signs in particular (Taurus,

Virgo, Capricorn) feel drawn towards.

All is one. This root chakra gives us the ability to provide for our self. We tend to hold a tremendous amount of fear here. This can block us from going forward. This is a space symbolising where we come from. The fear of being abandoned resides here. Everybody connected to this space reminds us of our spiritual and emotional connections.

This is the chakra that holds soulmates together.

Past Connections

Although our spiritual and physical journey is about connection, the connections to all family matters within this space can be here to teach us the most difficult lessons. Walking away from a very hurtful situation takes huge strength and courage. Such decisions are basically about uprooting yourself and separating yourself from any pain you are feeling.

Only you know how you feel. We will never know what brought a particular person to hurt you, or the hurt you inflicted upon others. Remember, whatever you did was what you felt was right at that moment, and where you were energetically at that time.

This root chakra is connected to past events.

If you are an Earth sign – Taurus, Virgo or Capricorn – your lessons will be deep-rooted. You have come here to feel that hurt and pain physically and / or emotionally through the people closest to you.

To get to a place of understanding and to a higher perspective of love takes time. Earth signs want to take it slowly to understand why. When it comes to understanding yourself as a spiritual being having a human experience, realising that your experiences were always part of your soul contract is not an easy pill to swallow. As you unfold into understanding, you will be rewarded from your higher self and will step into who you were always meant to be.

Working with and clearing blockages from the root chakra will help you to achieve this.

Also, people will come into your life to help you. This idea can be difficult to understand, and the process can take time as you may be carrying issues from a past life. This chakra is about deep roots. It's closely connected to people, so when we work with this chakra and take the inward journey to find out who we are, we may disconnect from people, places and things. This is necessary as it allows us to make the connection to self. In order for anything to grow it needs solid roots. Be courageous, be brave. Put in the hard work and with sheer determination you will make it right.

This chakra can go out of alignment when your sense of trust and safety is threatened. By working with it, you can reconnect to the here and now, enter a space of where you are and who you are, and rise up from the ashes.

When you make the decision to work on this chakra, this is the starting point as you are laying the foundations for later work on the other six chakras. Take your time with this chakra – it is the making or breaking of your core essence. Remember, it is a process like everything else we face in life.

1st chakra is a single digit, where we are alone to start our journey of life.

Clairalience

Enables us with the gift of smelling. It's a very subtle and unique gift that allows us to smell odours or fragrances when connecting to spirit – we may sense a strong smell that we associate with somebody in particular. When I am working with Ms Takata, one of my Reiki ascendant masters, I sense a smell of floral perfume. This tells me she has entered the room and is ready to work with me. Ever get a smell that reminds you of a person or place? You were meant to smell it, to evoke a memory. Or for it to remind you of somebody that connects you to a certain time and place.

How to Strengthen Your Clairalience

Grounding your energy and working with your foundations to keep yourself strong and rooted whilst taking in different aromas is a wonderful way to enhance this skill. People who work with oils and herbs have strong roots within themselves. I would also imagine that chefs would be naturally gifted in this skill, too. We can usually relate smells to certain people in our life. If strong-smelling perfumes or aftershave bother you and give you headaches, clairalience is a psychic ability you will find easy to tap into.

Smelling scents of frankincense, nag champa or myrrh for no physical reason, usually suggests that high vibrational Spirits and Guides are near you and are bringing you spiritual gifts to help you with something.

Any floral smells could suggest a loved one is near.

Lilies and roses have distinct smells that are letting you know that Spirit is watching over you.

It can also happen that if you smell horrible scents for no physical reason, such as rotten eggs or meat, just something disgusting, this suggest the opposite: you need to remove yourself from this space. Form a bubble of protection around you by envisioning this and leave.

Dogs and cats have a heightened sense of smell which can give them an awareness to detect diseases within the human body, such as cancer. When this happens, they may "alert" by sniffing (dogs) or licking (cats) an area of your body. This intrigued me and I thought it may be helpful for you to know. Your sense of smell could be as accurate as a police dog's, if you're willing to spend time enhancing it.

Sometimes I find myself sneezing in my healing room for no apparent reason other than Spirit trying to communicate. I get distinctive smells from time to time that make me or my client sneeze. This is when Spirit uses your heightened psychic sense of smelling. You may smell different fragrances that are attached to the person you are working with.

As you come to develop this psychic ability, doing ground work with the root chakra will allow this spiritual gift to flourish for you. Spend time with different aromas. Unfamiliar scents can be caused by the energies, thoughts and emotions of other people. You will work towards understanding the differences of energies. The more you connect to people, the more scents you will pick up.

Basically, positive energies, thoughts, and emotions are going to smell good.

Negative energies, thoughts, and emotions will smell bad.

You could meditate upon smells such as grass, flowers, trees, a forest – smells that would have a spiritual source – and tune into your intuition and see what the smell is telling you.

A good exercise would be to ask a friend to blindfold you and bring you different smells of food or other things – good and bad things – and put them in front of you. Make a note of how your body responds to each smell, whether you feel an emotion or a sensation, and how you visualise the smell.

Signs You May be Clairalient
- You have smelled something that isn't around you
- You have a highly developed sense of smell generally
- You can easily imagine how something smells
- You smell food before you eat it
- Certain smells change your mood or bring back fond memories
- You relate smells to certain people in your life

If you recognise yourself in four or more of the above, chances are you have the gift of clairalience.

Affirmations to Increase Your Clairalience
- I am observing smell and odours more often and am connecting with them through the Universe, which offers me meaning through the experience of remembering.
- I recall past memories through my sense of smell.
- This superpower will assist me with the unfolding of all my natural gifts.

Clairgustance:
Clear Sense of Taste

Sacral Chakra

This chakra is connected to our sense of taste (savour your food).

Open yourself up to some new foods! One way to stimulate your sense of taste is to taste citrus fruits. This will encourage your tastebuds to go into overdrive. Whilst working and clearing this chakra you will find that, as you progress, different tastes will randomly be sensed.

This chakra is connected to the element of water. It deals with pleasure and is blocked by guilt. It's located just below your naval, above the root chakra.

Holding on to guilt from past events may cause a blockage in your system, preventing you from moving forward. As the chakra deals with pleasure, make sure you have some fun along the way while clearing and balancing this chakra.

Conscious awareness level starts around seven years of age and is fully developed by fourteen years.

All our emotional connections from childhood to adulthood are stored here – this chakra is a resting place for stored emotions. This is the centre where we improve our relationship with ourselves and others.

Its energy colour is orange, and its mantra / seed sound is VAM. Chanting this sound and visualising this colour helps you channel your full focus and awareness to this energy centre within your body.

Honour this space within you that holds your emotional connection to self. Honour one another. This is our holy grail, where we create life. Our creative juices are here and are usually blocked by fear of abandonment. Remember, our journey through this life is one of connection – we are never alone.

This is also a space in which we can hold negative feelings.

Lessons from ALL our relationships are stored here.

All water signs (Cancer, Scorpio and Pisces) are deeply connected to this chakra and to our moon cycles. You have come here to learn the importance of the emotional attachments we all have to each other, people, places and things. These are forever moving. Your journey involves learning to let go of any attachments that don't serve your higher good. You will feel this deeply when others are disconnecting from you and when you are disconnecting from others, so be protective of your space and who you allow into your circle of care and trust.

All loss, hurt and pain memory is held here within the sacral chakra. Water IS memory – so the water babies, Cancer, Scorpio and Pisces, may find it a little more difficult to process these things as they are like intuitive sponges – they are constantly picking up on the energy they are surrounded by and sometimes don't understand why. They love to reminisce on old times and are extremely sensitive souls.

However, water is unpredictable and can change at a moment's notice – so watch out. The Cancerian will retreat back under their shell to protect their energy and their family; the Scorpion will sting you – or, worse still, sting themselves – should you cross them. The Piscean, well they will just watch the show that is unfolding in front of them, and let it all go with the flow.

The sacral chakra deals with the exploration of things that give us pleasure: family, friends, music, food, art, nature and intimacy, to name but a few.

When this chakra is in balance, we feel special, loved and connected to everyone and everything. Our needs and desires are balanced with a healthy sensuality. If we find ourselves disconnected, we feel emotionally unstable, lack control over our physical desires, and have a fear of being seen and being vulnerable. If you feel this way, work to balance your sacral chakra.

This is chakra number 2, so we are no longer alone. It's about relationships, teamwork, coming together, romance, companionship, duality, joining forces with one another.

How to Strengthen Your Clairgustance

Set your intention to spend time practising some mindful eating. Maybe go for a meal, invite your personal Spirit Guide to come along, order something that you feel drawn towards, pay attention to the different variations of taste that each food brings.

You may find that tasting has a powerful effect on you and evokes some strong emotions, making you feel sad, happy, nostalgic or even homesick. Even revisiting the memory of a holiday abroad can evoke a certain taste of food or wine that you had. When tasting anything, or recalling a taste, ask yourself: what do you feel?

Try to imagine different flavours – for instance, a lemon. What might you feel when you taste it? The texture, its juice, its skin etc. Does it leave a sour taste in your mouth?

Ask your Guides to help you distinguish what taste means for you as you strengthen this rare psychic connection of clairgustance. It is a very powerful and rare ability. Personally, I have never been great at exploring new tastes but food definitely can evoke some strong emotions for people.

Have you a relationship with your food? Can you relate food to memories? Once again, as with the gift of clairalience, I feel that chefs would be really good at being able to tap into this one. They have a natural skill that allows them to taste different ingredients in food.

If you are meditating and are calm and relaxed and / or working with somebody, try to imagine different flavours. If there is a particular food or taste you loved, try to visualise it. Remember, you are strengthening your focus on taste and working with Spirit – they are never far from you. You could ask your Spirit team / Guides to assist you with giving you tastes that they enjoyed, and what you might taste when they are around.

If you experience this, it could be Spirit trying to communicate with you through this psychic ability.

If you are trying to enhance this skill, always set your intention by trying new food and savouring the taste. Ask your Guide to help you with remembering through taste, assisting you with allocating the taste to a memory that you may have forgotten and why it became your favourite food in the first place.

The two lower chakras link up your physical senses of (smell) clairalience, and (taste) Clairgustance. When we make a link with taste to a childhood memory, we can usually smell the food also. Again, these psychic abilities can be a little harder to improve as they are connected to lower chakra work. This would be deep-dive work, where we concentrate our thoughts on particular memories which evoke long-forgotten hidden senses to come up to the surface of remembrance.

Remember, everything you do still has to come up from these spaces right through your heart chakra. You are remembering love with no boundaries, just truths of the good, bad and indifferent of times shared. It is in your *now* that you are choosing to "go there" to investigate how to tap into clearing these senses in order to identify why you may be experiencing certain tastes, and to develop your clairgustance.

Signs You May be Clairgustant

- You have strong memories of how something tastes.
- Being surrounded by good-smelling things is important to you.
- Scents can bring you into a space of calm and happiness.
- You get food cravings for no apparent reason.
- You love cooking and trying different tastes.

Affirmations to Increase Your Clairgustance

- I will choose to spend time savouring my food.
- I will introduce myself to a variety of new tastes.
- I have a good healthy relationship with food.
- I have a strong connection with taste and will start to acknowledge an emotion or memory that taste evokes for me of different places, people and things.

Clairsentience:
Gut Feelings

Solar Plexus Chakra

This chakra is connected to our sense of sight. "What you see is what you get" springs to mind. To stimulate your sight, try contemplating on some sacred art – perhaps studying an object such as a crystal, flower or candle then closing your eyes and seeing if you can visualise it in your mind's eye. Visualising is key to connecting, opening new channels within the mind, offering you new possibilities and opportunities.

This chakra deals with willpower, strength and trust, and is blocked by shame.

Its energy colour is yellow and its mantra / seed sound is RAM. Chanting this sound and visualising this colour helps you channel your focus and awareness to this energy centre within your body.

The element it is connected to is fire.

Conscious awareness comes in from the age of fourteen and is fully developed by the age of twenty-one.

This chakra symbolises our sun within, our light. This is where our authentic self lies, our gut, our movement, our instinct. Just like the sun in the sky, this chakra is activated when the sun rises every day. A new day, a new dawn. Appreciate the sunsets, too, for rest and rejuvenation. Find solace within yourself in the silence and darkness.

This is where we take off the labels and different hats we wear, to find out who we truly are. Just like the pealing of an onion, we go through and into the layers of self.

The fire signs of Aries, Leo and Sagittarius are deeply connected to this chakra. They come here to find / replenish their light within as they give so much of their light to others; to find their willpower and strength and the courage to move forward gracefully from hurtful situations.

Just like fire, our fire signs like to move and can find it difficult to be still. So, don't be hard on yourself if you are a fire sign and can't contain that flame – your form of meditation can be done through movement. Your lessons in life are to have confidence and strength and to shine brightly in everything you do. Your personality is magnetic and everybody will be naturally drawn to your light.

We can all go through difficult phases as we find our way in the big world of chaos. We are a mixture of many different energies and standing up for ourselves can be difficult if we feel vulnerable and are trying to get on with different people with their own opinions and perspectives on life. It can get confusing for us as we may not be sure how to express ourselves, but we find our way through it, and seek out people who hold the same views and vibration as us, giving us that sense of understanding and belonging.

We are literally carrying the flame and keeping it going can be draining when some people you meet take some of your light for themselves. We sure as hell don't understand how we work energetically at this stage – but difficulties teach us much about life through the people we are destined to meet along the way.

This chakra is all about our gut instincts and the connections we all share to one another. We become emotionally attached to everyone, and unfortunately the world keeps turning and people, places and things change – this is a lesson in itself. On a cellular level we are also changing every day, our biology is changing, and everyone around us is changing, too.

Our solar plexus reminds us of our confidence, it's the seat of our personal power, where we find our True Self. We can all get caught up in different labels of "who", we are supposed to be, either following tradition, or going our own way. Here, in the solar plexus chakra, is where you take off the labels and come out of that line, and cross over to the other side of the road, being noticed, being heard and being your authentic self. You can be whoever you want to be. Being your authentic self will never steer you wrong. It can prove difficult at first because we are conditioned to talk, do and be a certain way due to the expectations of others but it is always worth being true to ourselves.

Try and embrace every part of you that holds you back. Feeling criticised, judged and / or being rejected are the biggest contributors of a blocked solar plexus. If this is how you feel, work on unblocking this chakra by igniting that fire in your belly. Know your self-worth, and build your self-confidence to regain your body's strength and re-balance your self.

This is chakra number 3. This is where we manifest from – our creative flow mixed in with our desire, drive and passion to do what we love and what we feel drawn towards.

Igniting that inner flame is about combining your story with your glow and flow. When this chakra is balanced, the artist within you will reappear to manifest your desires.

How to Strengthen Your Clairsentience
Ask for signs – talk with your Guides in the same way you would have every-day conversations with other real people. Ask them to guide you and help you with improving and heightening your solar plexus and heart chakra awareness – they will give you signs everywhere if you're open enough to receive them. It's like a game of treasure hunt, but you

can't go looking – the signs will be placed in front of you! From people you meet and talk to, to places you find yourself in by chance, to what you hold in your hands.

I know it sounds kinda weird, but it gets easier over time to understand this concept.

The colour that can help you strengthen this ability is yellow as it's associated with your solar plexus. Yellow is the colour of sunshine, of happiness; it is light and energising. Just by intentionally wearing this colour or eating food this colour, even wrapping yourself up in a yellow blanket, will invoke feelings of happiness and joy.

I'm not too familiar with crystals, but I have come to believe that citrine is a powerful crystal for opening, enhancing and healing this chakra's potential. It's a crystal that I would use. There are many crystals to choose from. You could just go into a crystal shop and feel which works for you; you'll know when you see it, you will feel it working with you straight away. I just trust what I'm drawn towards – usually, the colours associated with the chakras match up with crystals or stones.

Lavender and Rose oil are also good for rubbing into the solar plexus space with the intention of increasing your clairsentient gift.

Sending your concentration into these spaces within your body will also help with releasing blockages. The solar plexus is just below your rib cage. The more you connect to any of your energetic coloured wheels of light, the more your energy will flow within these spaces in your body.

You can open and strengthen this psychic ability of tapping into your gut feelings and your intuitive hits will get stronger. Setting your intention before you do any exercises is paramount for a good clear connection with yourself and your Guides.

Our counterpart thinking / logical mind will always get in the way of our intuition because we are conditioned to trust our head and ignore our heart. You've heard the expression "wearing your heart on your sleeve" – this is allowing yourself to be vulnerable with your emotions in an honest and open manner. If you wear your heart loosely on your sleeve, you are opening yourself to feel easily hurt or offended by others.

You heart has a rightful place in the centre of your chest and is in alignment with your brain. Your heart and brain must be best friends, creating a union within for you to achieve the maximum benefit from all your experiences. Trust your self.

The alignment of your mind, body and spirit takes shape in a place deep beneath the surface. Start practising not to take people's opinions personally. Remember, we are all built to be resilient. Just knowing we can work through anything offers us hope and a light at the end of every dark tunnel we have to go through. Trusting yourself and your gut instincts takes a HUGE amount of alone time and patience.

When it comes to solar plexus work, just as in real life, we will always have road blocks and barricades to cross and get through.

It's our instinct, our gut, our second brain that allows us to light up any darkness that falls upon us. Clairsentience is a psychic ability that we all share and is there to teach us all about how others make us feel, through the people that we are destined to meet along the way.

You don't just conjure those butterflies within, they don't just take flight in your stomach for no reason. Trust them.

Signs You May be Clairsentient

- Do you get physical gut feelings from people?
- You easily pick up on temperature changes in the room.
- You can feel it in your body when somebody is lying to you.
- You can sense subtle changes in the energy around you.
- You can sometimes physically feel other people's pain.
- You get physically ill when bad things are going to happen.
- You can physically feel the energy of Spirits.

Affirmations to Increase Your Clairsentience

- I am physically and emotionally strong.
- My mind, body and soul are in line with the energy of Mother Earth.
- I am putting positive energy back into the Earth.
- Thank you, Mother Earth, for this transfer of energy and for uplifting me physically.

Clairempathy:
Clear Sense of Touch

Heart Chakra

This chakra governs unconditional love and understanding the power of connection. It's no wonder it takes two keys to unlock its potential: a union of souls and seeds of love shared between you and another.

I see everybody as a key that can either block or assist you with unlocking your potential and opening yourself up to your innate psychic ability of clairempathy.

However, the gift of self-love, through a more meaningful connection with yourself, must come first in order for you to see yourself through the eyes of others. This starts with the unfolding of the heart chakra.

It is about opening yourself up to receive love and allow it in. Everything starts and ends with you, but in between we find different aspects of ourselves through others. We want to seek and find the good in every possible situation. Accessing the power of love within your self is huge; you will know when you are ready to accept and surrender to the forces of love and connection. Nothing can or will stand in your way. Those walls will break down, brick by brick, freeing you to be you once again.

This chakra is also connected to our sense of touch. For example, when practising massage or Reiki healing, concentrate on a light touch, stimulating both you and the recipient. You can feel energy through touch, even just holding hands. When you make physical contact with another person's skin, sense the energy coming into you.

We can easily shut down this clairempathy sense with a closed or blocked heart chakra. Our previous experiences teach us who or what to trust. Depending on our personal experiences, sometimes our edges can become tough and resistant towards the energy of love – to counteract that, learn to trust it. Allow love to come into you just as much as you allow it to flow from you, too. Start with you – that's it. Nobody else comes into this – this is your journey, your experience

Love is divine power. This chakra is our centre of love and compassion. It is connected to the element of air – no wonder love can simply take our breath away!

It activates from the age of twenty-one and is fully developed by the age of twenty-nine years.

The colour of this energy centre is green and its mantra / seed sound is YAM. Chanting this sound and visualising this colour helps you channel your full focus and awareness to this energy centre within your body.

This can be a rewarding, yet very painful, journey for the air signs Gemini, Libra and Aquarius, as they have come here to find compassion, love, acceptance and forgiveness within all experiences of the heart. This is a space that offers unconditional love. You will see the goodness through all hardship and have a flock of kindred spirits to lean on in times of need.

The heart chakra holds the most difficult of challenges to face, as there will be a lot of losses and hurtful disconnections will be made through difficult decisions. But through your faith and belief with being a natural visionary, you come to the table with a deep sense of natural trust of knowing it will be okay.

Heart chakra is a space that offers you solace and grace in times of hardship.

Issues related to this chakra include love, compassion, hope, commitment, fear of loneliness, grief, anger, the inability to forgive one's self. This is the powerhouse of the human energy field.

This chakra deals with love and is blocked by grief. Nobody escapes either.

Our heart chakra is all about our emotional connections, how we are really feeling beneath the surface.

Everything is constantly changing around and within us, which means energy is moving constantly, too; the whole yin and yang movement of change. We are manifested yang energy and the yin is the movement of the energy in and all around us. Just because we don't see it, doesn't mean it's not there. It's something that is felt and is perceived differently by everyone. Nobody else feels it the way you do; we are all different. That's what makes us unique individuals.

This is chakra number 4, where we learn patience, loyalty and trust. We are looking to add structure and some seriousness now with matters of the heart, having some order laced with vitality and compassion in our life. We learn valuable lessons of love, and what feels right compared to what feels off and wrong.

How to Strengthen Your Clairempathy

We all have different levels of empathy. Sometimes, through very difficult experiences or trauma, we can easily close this gift off. If you constantly state that you don't care or it doesn't matter, your body believes you don't care so it shuts down this centre of love. Only you understand your unique experiences, so only you will know if part of you feels shut down or shut off from others.

In physics you are a physical form that occupies a space in time and possesses "rest mass", which is a great deal! Your thoughts create feelings that matter within your form. Your feelings matter greatly upon your self. Being able to recognise and separate feelings from form is an ability that you can train yourself to improve. You give yourself the capacity to love yourself on a soul level, and that's when your clairempathy reaches new heights, taking your love above and beyond self.

It is having an awareness and understanding of other people's energy. We have to transcend any limiting beliefs we may hold, which offers us an understanding of how best to navigate any negative or restrictive experiences.

Therefore, we can all assist each other through healing. Any form of healing is self-love. Taking yourself into a meditative state and switching off from external influences allows you to open your heart chakra through conscious breath, be present with your emotions, and view all aspects of your story through the eyes of love for self. In this way you can invite whatever you need in that moment to fill any void you may be feeling.

Love and gratitude occupy the highest vibrational frequencies. They are your best friends. These – love and gratitude – are what you need to bring back into your awareness after any heartache, sorrow or grief.

The Archangels have specific roles should you require anything in particular when it comes to matters of the heart. Educate yourself: get to know them; this will bring them closer to you. When you allow yourself to be open to receiving love, you will feel yourself in a protective blanket of pure love, supported by the Universe.

Set your intention to feel the energy whilst with different people. Try to see everybody outside of you as an extension of self, see everybody through the eyes of love and connection. Tune into your feelings when you are around people. Start recognising and tuning into how things and places make you feel. Your sensitivity will swell as you work on opening up your heart space.

Listen to conversations from a place of non-judgement. When we are listening to inspirational or encouraging words this allows us to vibrate on a higher frequency, giving us the feel-good factor, taking us up from lower-vibrational conversations.

Our bodies remember everything, so if you feel a familiar feeling, you have probably already been through the experience, it's just repeating again with a different set of characters. The Universe will bring lessons back to you if you didn't "get it" first time round.

The heart chakra is located in the centre of your chest. Here, we learn just how deeply we feel everything, from a soul level of loss and detachment to a space of unconditional love: two sides of the same coin. We are learning powerful lessons during our time here. It has come to be my belief that we inhabit many lifetimes together. Seeing through the eyes of energy and vibration encourages us all to see from a heightened sense of awareness, turning any difficult time in our life into a beautiful lesson of love and hope.

This heart space is where we develop a healthy relationship with ourselves and those closest to us. It is a source of deep and profound truths that cannot be expressed in words.

We are connecting our physical existence with our emotional centre. When this chakra is in alignment you are surrounded by love and joy, and are connected to the world around you and everybody in it.

Our 4th chakra indicates the phase of our journey where we find love, where we add structure to our intentions and create a life for ourselves with a bond that will never leave us. This chakra acts like a bridge between body and spirit: a space where we become really present with how we absorb, feel and connect with the energy we are surrounded by.

Clairempathy and Clairsentience – Joining Forces

Both the heart and solar plexus chakras deal with our present self, present time and place. They are closely linked; when connected they can work in harmony, allowing you to access your clairsentience.

Therefore, clairempathy and clairsentience can join forces to complete what you feel from another person or situation. These abilities will help you will form you own opinion upon meeting new people, or entering new or old spaces. You may feel a range of different emotions, from being comfortable to being uncomfortable. Remember to be open minded – be grounded and as present in the moment as you can be with where you are and whom you are with. Learn to trust your gut and what intuitive hits you receive when you work in full awareness of both these psychic abilities.

Here are some examples of combining these abilities:

Your now is the only time you have. Yesterday is past, tomorrow is a place we are heading towards. Doing the best you can in your now leads you to brighter tomorrows.

When the two abilities are clear and unblocked you will be saying things like: "This doesn't feel right"; "I've a gut feeling…" You will have that instantaneous feeling where your gut becomes your internal compass. When spending time with people, notice how your gut responds. It is important that you go about your day as usual, but pay attention to your gut feelings. Start to understand what feels like yours. Ask yourself "are these feelings mine?" Or somebody else's?

Where is this coming from? Internal or external? How do you *feel*?

You may even pick up somebody else's personality, could be a colleague at work, a friend, a family member, somebody that you get to spend time with. Ever find yourself using an expression you wouldn't normally use when you're around different people? – this is normal. You are actually tapping into each other's energy.

A happy-go-lucky person will make you feel light, jovial and friendly.

An anxious person will make you feel like something's not right.

This is when your clairempathy and clairsentience are working in tandem. Your solar plexus will tighten up with your gut instincts, which then evokes feelings of being nervous, worried or, worse still, nauseated.

Gut feelings? We have all experienced this about a person or situation.

Ever walked into a room and thought, I don't have a good feeling about this scenario. Or speaking to somebody where your gut is vibrating and screaming, "something's not right!"

We've all experienced going into a space where we just know there's been an argument, or we're getting bad vibes – yet what we see suggests everything is fine, everybody's just going about their day, looking normal and smiling, but you could cut the tension with a knife. When you have a feeling about something not being right with the picture you see before you, trust your guts. Your clairempathy is working with your clairsentience. As the old saying goes – if something doesn't feel right, chances are it isn't.

If you were raised in a home where there wasn't a lot of truth, where there were family conflicts, parents constantly arguing and / or fighting, where you overheard conversations that you didn't understand, yet everything seemed good when you were in the room, and so you thought you were imagining it...you might just have a harder time trusting your gut and tapping into this ability.

However, if your parents sat you down, validated how you were feeling, were open and honest with you when things weren't great and let you know they were working through any problems together as a family, that is more likely to allow your psychic abilities of clairempathy and clairsentience to flourish and naturally become stronger.

You're not imagining it. There are energy walls and boundaries that people don't allow you to access. And this is okay. It's the same with a simple question that we ask each other every day: "How are you doing?"; "Are you all right?" Are most people going to go into a whole conversation about their deepest feelings with another person when they're just passing in the street? Probably not. The question is one of courtesy, politeness and kindness as we pass each other by.

Nobody knows what internal battle another is fighting, but I can assure you everyone is dealing with some chaos in their life. Being polite is like a mask we all wear. We give or receive the reassuring smile and nod back, even if we are carrying the world on our shoulders. We leave it at, "Yes, I'm good, thanks for asking…", or a simple smile. And so we close the door to a deeper conversation. This is also okay – this seems to be the norm in our society, wouldn't you agree?

So, being fully aware of these empathetic senses when tapping into them is vital, as is knowing when to switch it on or off, depending on your mind set, where you are or who you are with. The big question here for you is: Do you trust yourself? Because it all comes back to self-belief, self-worth and self-trust.

It can be a difficult one to get to grips with. Because self-worth is a huge issue. The truth is 95% of us feel we are not good enough, strong enough, worthy enough or brave enough to cross the lines that push us beyond our own energetic limitations and boundaries.

Improving your clairempathy for one another will increase and enhance your clairsentience ability. It is exactly the same as working on a muscle group in the gym to improve your physical body, except it's a spiritual muscle – you can strengthen it. It's as simple as just trusting your feelings.

For example, you're going about your day and somebody pops into your head and you're not sure why, but you feel something's not right – call them! When you are new at becoming intuitive, you will tend to be drawn to a negative aspect of something (our brain is trained to focus on the negative). Don't phone and put the creeps into them by asking, "Is there something's wrong?" or saying "I've a bad feeling…"

You can just say, "I've been thinking about you a lot today – everything okay?"

They may say everything is fine. The point is that you listened to your gut and reacted to the feeling of needing to make the connection.

I've personally had many experiences of something not feeling right, and brushed them off – not considering or understanding what was happening. It's only through meditation that I have revisited those feelings and was able to make the connections.

The divine lies within you. Your Guides (the Universe) will show you what you need to be shown to remind you of the emotions you felt during an experience where you felt something was "wrong", but brushed it off with a conditioned reaction that feels wrong to you in your now – this is when healing visits you.

Signs You May Have Clairempathy

- Any conflict can really upset you.
- You are extremely sensitive and easily overwhelmed around others.

- You can sense beyond our normal five senses.
- You can be exhausted easily.
- You have a strong desire to be alone.
- You feel a strong sense of emotions whilst watching some TV programmes.
- You have a strong connection with nature.

Conflict is a very important part of every relationship. Without healthy arguments with family, friends or spouses, issues can become greater than they actually are. It's important to work on how you deal with conflict and how you can express yourself without draining your energy. People with overpowering energies that come from a space of being all-knowing and "better than" can drain you of your vitality, making you feel small, weak and unsupported.

You may feel it's not worth the argument and let things slide. But if something is important to you, it's never too late to set new boundaries of what's acceptable and what's not. If you come from a space of love, there will be total understanding. If there is fear, there will be resistance. The internal battle of what feels right and wrong for you will take centre stage within your heart space. Your Intuition will flourish when you begin the process of understanding the gift of clairempathy.

Affirmations to Increase Your Clairempathy
- I am transforming into someone who is unafraid to find my "true self".
- Expressing my emotions is improving the way I feel.
- It's important that I stand up for myself and voice my opinion.
- I allow myself to be seen, and stand up for what I believe in whilst developing the courage to stand up for and be myself.

Clairaudience:
Clear Sense of Hearing

Throat Chakra

This chakra is connected to our sense of hearing. To stimulate this centre, listen to some music – classical, piano, meditative sounds. Singing songs or chanting are also a great way to bring calm to this chakra's serene quality.

In this phase in our life we understand the importance of the spoken word.

Our conscious awareness level starts around the age of twenty-nine and reaches its full potential by the age of thirty-five.

Imagine that. Yes, of course we have spoken and expressed ourselves much earlier, but I feel this gift grows as we learn from our life experiences and realise the importance of our words and the impact they have on people.

This chakra deals with truth and is blocked by lies.

Communication is a gift from above.

In the beginning was 'the Word'; it created the world.

Issues related to this chakra include choice and strength, criticism, faith, knowledge, following your dreams, personal expression, even the ability to release your personal will to the divine, which offers you guidance along the way. We hold a tremendous amount of energy in this chakra. Each time we don't speak our truth and don't say how we feel, we swallow our feelings and they find a way back into our system.

When the energy is balanced in this area, we mean what we say and say what we mean. Saying what you want to say at any given moment is a whole lot easier! This energy centre speaks for itself. It is our centre of truth.

What's your internal truth? Your internal dialogue can take time and patience to understand. Sorry does seem to be hardest word to say. But by apologising for your war of words with anyone you hurt intentionally or unintentionally takes huge bravery – not a lot of people are able to do this. Staying silent is a natural knee-jerk reaction when we come from a space of hurt, it's like a form of protection. Count yourself lucky if you received an apology from anybody that knows they hurt you.

The throat chakra can open a whole can of worms, bringing it into alignment is HUGE. Sometimes we don't like to admit when we are wrong, or to acknowledge any mistakes we've made. We are only human. But admitting to your mistakes can often free you from any torment you may be carrying. It can have a ripple effect on your whole system.

The throat chakra is connected to our higher self and works with Spirit when opened and aligned to receive. It's good to talk.

This psychic ability allows us to hear Spirit.

This is apparent when we use sentences such as: "Did you hear that?"; "Talk to me"; "I hear you"; "I am here"; "I am listening".

Hearing Voices

It's very common to hear others' voices within the mind – you may have random names come into your head for no apparent reason; happens all the time. It's important to listen to and to trust your own inner voice.

You may hear a random song that keeps playing in your mind. That's a sign that you should pull up the lyrics and read them, and listen to the song – because there is something in this for you. Ever wake up singing a song? This is very common when you start to improve this clairaudient skill – or you wake up thinking about the title of a book you should read, or a poem. Ever read a book and you can give different characters different voices? This is absolutely a great way to jump-start this ability!

A note of caution: developing your clairaudience can sometimes cause great confusion and can be confused with mental illness or a disorder of the mind. Some disorders can be disabling, impairing daily functions, and can have a significant impact on your ability to work, study or perform daily tasks. People with these disorders may hear voices in their head and this can have a very negative impact on their day-to-day life. If you are prone to this kind of illness / disorder, remember always to discuss any course of action with your doctor before undertaking any change or doing any exercises to enhance your clairaudience.

The difference when you link to Spirit is that the experience is kind and comforting in a validating way. The internal voice of your intuitive clairaudience is one that encourages you, offers you insight, guidance and wisdom, and links with your intuition. That voice will never be a scary or frightening experience. It's totally the opposite – it's kind, calm and instructive.

You will always hear a clear and gentle tone when you are hearing clairaudient information, rather than a negative narrative, which can sometimes signal the onset of mental illness. However, be aware that it can cause confusion – so take your time with this one and always put your health – physical and mental – and wellbeing first.

You can strengthen this psychic ability by allowing yourself time in silence. Listening to nature's sounds – birdsong, the wind in the trees, ocean sounds…all these things work, too. This helps to get your body near high-frequency tones that feel right and bring you into a vibrational match that offers you teachings from higher realms. When you sit in silence with nature, you are preparing your body to become a vessel for higher levels of understanding.

Spirit Guides and information can't come to you if you are not quiet. I know this can seem hard 'cause it's such a busy world full of noise. But it can be done.

Start with small doses of being alone and just breathing. The yappy dog mind we all have sometimes will continue to tell you that you have things to do, that you can't be sitting around doing nothing. Don't let that voice prevent you from being still. Acknowledge the yappy dog within and tell it: I am breathing, I am breathing…eventually, the yappy dog will not bother you because it now knows you're not listening – and eventually a small voice within you that's clear and calm will reach you. You can then begin conversations that are fresh, new, informative and insightful!

Our 5th chakra is like the wildcard because our words and thoughts hold energy. When we change the way we express ourselves – for example, asking instead of demanding and / or expecting – this invokes mammoth changes within us and helps us to listen to and adapt to the perspectives and opinions of others. It helps us to be open to listening rather than judging. It helps us to stay impartial. Through listening, we are learning.

Internal conflicts and self-sabotage can close this chakra's potential for growth. Change comes with new vibrational tones. So, if you feel you need to balance this part of your self, or if you want to improve your clairaudience ability, work with this chakra.

How to Strengthen Your Clairaudience
Chanting this mantra is really good for opening up the throat chakra – its mantra / seed sound is HAM, meaning "I am sound, therefore I

speak". It is a gift to have this ability. Your words hold energy – being aware of your words and the delivery of them will have a profound effect upon your whole system. Say nice things to yourself!

This chakra is associated with the colour blue. When you are working on this chakra, be consciously aware by wearing blue, eating blue. Wearing a scarf to protect your throat will also work, once you're intentionally focusing on it.

Chanting the sound HAM, and visualising the colour blue, helps you channel your full focus and awareness to this energy centre within your body, located at the base of your neck.

Use whatever affirmations resonate with you to stretch open this energy vortex. Setting your intention, concentrating and focusing your awareness on this space for spirit to work through you is a great start.

Our human body consists of four elements: earth, water, fire and the rest is ether. The throat chakra represents the element of ether. Ether represents the space in and around you, whereas the other three elements remain constant but the percentage of Ether can be enhanced. Each element is responsible for different structures in the body. Ether can be expressed within the empty spaces. It's referred to as the element as potentiality: learning to express our self through sound and vibration.

There are no zodiac signs that correspond to this because it is about freedom of expression; the potential for us all to connect. A quote from the late Robin Williams always stayed with me when I began this work: "Everybody talks about finding their voice. If you do your homework, your voice will find you!"

This is so true.

Remember, you are your own boss, the CEO of your own life. Do whatever works for you in order to get you through your day without losing yourself in a story that's not part of why you are here right now. Don't get caught up with the drama of everybody's else life. What's important is the life you are creating. It's not about where you have been, it's about where you are going.

You can get crystals that help with opening your throat chakra, perhaps a necklace with a crystal hanging in the centre, where this energy vortex is. This is a great tip for starting out with throat chakra work to improve your clairaudience.

Listening is a skill, remaining focused on the information coming into you needs concentration. You might find yourself drifting when listening to some conversations. If you catch yourself doing this, inhale and come back into listening. There is a message within all that talking for you – we are all delivering messages to one another! Your awareness of conversations happening around you is important because these are keys to doorways within your psyche.

In this line of business (writing about and teaching Reiki) using and understanding the power of words is hugely important for anyone who wants to share their work. It can be difficult to explain something or express what you feel. Your mind can become full of information and images that may not make any sense, although someone out there needs to read or hear the message. Your job is to ensure the message does make sense, so readers understand it.

For instance, I am sitting here at my desk, where I do have a link with Spirit; this is me working with my clairaudience ability. I will read back what I have written when I take a break and, to be honest, I sometimes think, wow – did I write that!

It makes more sense when I write it and even more sense when I read it.

I never knew that I had this ability before I did any of this work –

it just happened when I started to unblock channels within my sacral chakra. That allowed me to express how I was feeling and my creative juices started to flow into the pages of the diaries I was writing!

Writing something down is way easier that speaking it, so that's why I decided to do only short videos online for grounding – baby steps!

I sometimes find that I get totally jumbled up with words when I feel Spirit is working with me – the words and images can come in so quickly that the doesn't make sense or I find myself talking really fast. I know, over time I will find that medium within me that will allow me to express slowly and clearly just like I hear it in my head.

As I write, I am literally allowing what's coming into my head to go down into my hands – exactly what I do when healing – it's pure light! Fast as light, too. I could have a couple of hundred words done within minutes. It just flows.

So, when I teach, I have already written down how I am going to explain it to students – it's how I roll, I'm okay with that. When I first started teaching this way, I felt it was wrong, that I should adlib – that's the perfectionist in me. I don't want to forget to mention something, or for students to miss out on anything, so by writing it down first I know I definitely won't forget! That way I know you will have all the information you need in whatever timeframe we have together.

When using your intuitive skills, you can have the strongest and most profound experiences. However, the downside to it is when working on your intuition you can doubt yourself. Our biggest critic resides within. Fear and self-doubt will play a huge part in you "thinking" you're wrong. And you will question it always – this is the nature of figuring out what feels right or wrong. So you've got to hold onto the times when you get it right. How it makes you feel in that moment – how does your body affirm this for you? Remember that feeling. This is a huge part of doing this work.

With clairaudience you could start by hearing something from within. Then you could see something that might throw you off balance – this is when we experience a sensory overload. Our mind can become completely scrambled, so aim to focus on only one thing at a time. Just like when doing chakra work, we need to break it down. One day at a time is a great start. The Clairaudient would say "Did you hear that?"…Nope, I didn't hear that but you know what you heard – maybe your name being called? – so trust it. Trust yourself.

Although clairaudience is primarily about hearing, automatic writing is also a very powerful spiritual practice that supports your personal connection to the divine.

Take a moment to clear your mind. In your own time, imagine your crown chakra opening and allowing the clear white beam of light down through your whole being, all the way down to the floor. Imagine your roots anchoring your thoughts as you become mindful of peace and calm.

Ask for somebody you know that has crossed over to step forward and work through you as they write you a love letter, maybe a memory that only you two share. Don't think about it, just start writing. Allow your pen to become a microphone and let your Spirit Guide work through you. This works in allowing you to be present with your thoughts.

Signs You May be Clairaudient

- You hear external voices that others don't.
- You love music or play a musical instrument.
- You talk to yourself.
- You are an auditory learner.
- You had imaginary friends as a child.
- You mentally and emotionally need quiet time to yourself.
- Your internal voice says random words, names or statements.

Affirmations to Increase Your Clairaudience

- I trust my intuition and the gifts I have been given.
- I am open to the messages I am supposed to hear.
- My inner voice is strong.
- Spirit Guides, please help me in my Clairaudience journey, open my mind to the messages I need to hear from you to guide me on my journey.

Clairvoyance:

Seeing Clearly; Understanding

The Third Eye Chakra

This chakra is our command centre.

This is the eye that allows us to go within and explore all the lower chakras within our psyche. Our conscious awareness of this eye opening is from the age of thirty-five to forty-two years. This is a time of deep evaluation of life and your journey.

This chakra's colour is a deep indigo and it is connected to supreme light. Your soul tries to connect with you through this light.

Connected to our sixth sense, our inner eye allows us to explore our universe within. To stimulate this centre, practise skills which require your intuition, such as divination tools: tarot, Reiki healing, runes, crystals, meditation. These allow you to be open to receive any information that may be coming in to you.

This chakra deals with insight and is blocked by illusion.

Its mantra / seed sound is OMM. Chanting this sound and visualising the colour indigo helps you channel your full focus and awareness to this energy centre, which is located between the brows.

There are no zodiac signs allocated to the upper chakras from the throat upwards as they are connected to your future self. What is it you foresee for yourself moving forward? This chakra's potential paves the way, creating all your dreams and turning them into your reality.

This is the eye that sees everything that is hidden within us, the illusion that is our story, that unfolds for us as we work through our chakra system.

The people we met, the stories, the laughter we shared, the pain we endured, the knockdowns, the upheavals, the changes, our spiritual growth, knowledge and understanding – everything comes together here.

We can revisit any space any time – any memory – and can change our story by simply making the changes we want to see in ourselves and living accordingly.

This is where you feel connected to yourself and the Universe. Your story gets unified here with a deep-rooted trust. Whatever choice you make at this stage of your journey will of course be the right one – there was never a wrong choice. Maybe a bad decision here and there, but we all have those. Those experiences brought you the best lessons and are a gentle reminder of who you are and who you are not.

When this chakra is balanced, you have a heightened sense of self.

The third eye holds the bridge between our mental and emotional perceptions of the world. This chakra works in partnership with the crown chakra to complete the "circuit". Working with these chakras is when we reach a new level of awareness and understanding.

How to Strengthen Your Clairvoyance
One way is by visualising and being creative with your ideas, bringing them into form. Following through with your decisions, seeing the bigger picture for yourself. This is you working with your intuitive centre, which will awaken and enhance your clairvoyance.

Focus your attention on nothing, allowing your thoughts to pass you by whilst being still with yourself. Notice what feelings begin to surface.

Stare at a candle for several moments until your eyes get lazy, then close your eyes and visualise the candle flame within your mind's eye. Keeping that image can prove difficult – but with practice it will get easier.

Whilst in meditation you can revisit your childhood home, if you want. Notice every detail: start at the front door, the step, the porch – what's to your right and what's to your left? Take your time remembering. Knock on the door and wait to see who welcomes you in, or simply open the door yourself. You have the key to access this space and place of remembrance. Walk inside and stand in the hallway and soak in everything that you see, bring everything back to life, in real time. The floor, the carpet, the wallpaper, the doors, the pictures – stop and soak it all in. This can be a very powerful exercise: you working with your intuitive centre to awaken your clairvoyance.

Clairvoyance: Clear Seeing; A Knowing
This is the psychic ability that allows you to see something in your mind's eye. You could just have a really good imagination, maybe it was something you watched on the television the other night or a story that you listened to…or perhaps you should trust your self.

Clairvoyance can be really hard to fully develop. I reckon a lot of people have the ability naturally – tending to be very right-brained. Creative people have wonderful imaginations: artist, writers, poets. Whilst having the ability to be creative or imaginative helps us strengthen our clairvoyant abilities, we can easily pass it off as our imagination.

Then we can start saying things like – "Do you see what I mean?" and "Can you see what I'm talking about?" In writing this, I am also learning to enhance this psychic connection.

When tuning into your clairvoyance, you may see a memory from your own life that is relevant for the information you are trying to get: an image of a friend, or a symbol that might be common – that you are shown again and again. Recognising this can be hard, too, as you have to understand what that symbol means to you.

For instance, a yellow rose may hold a significant meaning for you, if you are shown it – or it may be significant for the person you are with. There's a familiarity there within your memory, so this is when you blend your intuition with it.

A red rose could mean new romance and love coming for you, or for someone else it could signify a lost love.

A snake might represent someone is being sneaky for one person, whereas it could represent rebirth for another. If you're being shown a symbol, focus on it, bring it to life in your mind and hold it for as long as you can, connecting it to a memory, a card, a chakra or a colour.

Do what will work for you.

Having a diary to collect your thoughts with images would be incredibly useful as you create a symbolic dictionary that you place into your third eye chakra – again, remember to practise patience with your self within this territory of learning.

I often have great visualisations within my Reiki Room doing healing as I concentrate on the body part / area and the light pouring into that space from my hands. The room suddenly comes alive with the great energetic visual I am receiving.

Any concentration exercises or techniques that allow you to focus and light up your third-eye chakra are worth doing on a regular basis because they help you to go within for the answers you seek.

Many people think if you're clairvoyant that you walk around seeing dead people – this is not the case, it's the ability to see things within your mind's eye, the exact same as when you see people, places and things within your imagination – that's why it's misunderstood.

It can be the most difficult gift to trust.

Signs You May be Clairvoyant

- You have vivid dreams and you remember them.
- You can see Auras.
- You have visual flashes of images.
- You find it easy to visualise things.
- You are a visual learner.
- You are drawn to beautiful landscapes.
- You had an imaginary friend as a child.
- You seem to have a natural sense of direction.
- You sometimes have visions of the past, present or future.

Affirmations to Increase Your Clairvoyance

- I am clairvoyant, my inner visions are crystal clear.
- I am a clear channel with increased psychic awareness.
- I trust the images and information I am receiving.
- I see energy clearly, easily and effortlessly.

Our 6th chakra assists with our development that can connect us to our higher self, which to me, is our future self. Visualisation is a key factor here, where your imagination meets your creation, where you take that leap of faith into understanding yourself as a spiritual being. This chakra takes us back into remembering our story, revisiting where we feel everything and heal. Chakra number six can take us back in time to revisit our past or to travel forward.

Claircognizance:
A Clear Knowing

Crown Chakra

This chakra is our Cosmic Connection to the Divine.

This is your centre of Union. A space of oneness from all that you are to all that is.

This chakra is not related to a specific sense but it processes all the information that comes in from the other chakras, representing the highest state of chakra development possible.

It deals with Cosmic Energy and is blocked by ego attachment.

The colour I associate with this chakra is a cosmic light, sparkles of gold and white light; I see it just like stardust. You will come across different colours for this chakra, mostly purple. This is where the white light enters into us when we connected and present to the divine within.

Its mantra seed sound is AHH and / or OMM. Chanting these sounds and visualising white light from cosmic energy streaming into your crown chakra helps you channel your focus and awareness to this energy centre.

Finally, we have reached our final chakra connected to our journey as a human being. This is when we reach a greater understanding of life and our journey, cosmically connected to all that is. A union of both our feminine and masculine aspects, joining together into this beautiful enchanted tree of life!

We come into the level of consciousness of this chakra from the age of forty-two to forty-nine years of age. And this, my friends, is when the unfolding takes shape on our being. Your edges may have become tougher throughout your story, but this is when you really should soften and realise you are part of something much bigger than you can comprehend.

This chakra is the most remarkable instrument with infinite storage for carrying the whole world in our mind! The message with this chakra and this level of consciousness is to simply trust your feelings.

When something doesn't feel right, ask your "self" the questions you need answered. Don't discount the infinite power within you. Make the choice you need to make and work towards *your goals, your dreams*!

Within this space – this chakra of understanding – we have love and compassion for everybody who has crossed our life path, and for everybody's life path we have crossed, too. Immense healing for your whole system starts and ends here. It is the completion of who you are and what you have come here to do.

Your life has meaning and purpose; don't waste another minute of not living in joy. We are only travellers, travelling through space and time for such a short period of time. Leave your blueprint here, sign the invisible universal wall...*Ann was here*! Write that book that's in you.

The crown chakra is also the most vulnerable of the chakras because it is our direct line to source energy. Learn to maintain that flow of energy within your crown chakra, and you will see your life's purpose become so much clearer.

When things go wrong in life, as much as we want to scream and shout about it and tell everybody whose fault it was, this is when you take full responsibility for your own actions, whenever you had the choice to accept or decline, of saying yes or no. There was never a wrong turn – you were always meant to be there and then, just as you are meant to be where you are here and now. Your journey was always meant to lead you to this moment, where you are reading these words.

This is part of what I wrote earlier about our "Awakening", where we cast off our layers of conditioning about how we perceive energy. Remember, hold the desire within you to feel special and loved. Never lose that; that's where our hope lives. Sometimes, we may lose our grip on hope. But it always remains; it's part of everybody's blueprint, so it will never go too far. Always leave the light on and hold space for it within you.

We may break from time to time but we always find our way back home to love. Love is an eternal truth that we all share and can connect to. You are the major role-player within your story and life – it all starts and ends with you: you're unique in every sense, as I've said before.

Just be who you are. Trust where life is taking you, collect those golden nuggets of happiness and hold onto them as deep reminders of who you are, and what gifts you already possess that allow you to tap into your purpose.

Whether you are a healer, astrologist, intuitive reader, psychic, medium, read tarot cards, angel cards – whatever you are working with, these do help strengthen your intuitive abilities, which is a heightened understanding of energy.

How to Strengthen Your Claircognizance

This one is hard to work with as it represents a clear knowing.

We don't know how we know; we just know.

And we can encounter major self-doubt about what we "know".

When we are working with the crown chakra and coming from this space of claircognizance, the language would be:

"I knew that was going to happen"; "I know what's going on". Go investigate when you feel this – you are never wrong when you just know. It just sits with you.

Relate? Yes, we all can relate to this – but trusting ourselves is a mammoth task! After all, evidential mediumship is a real thing. We ask for evidence to know that they are really there. Mediums, believe it or not, are the biggest sceptics. We are definitely more surprised if we get it right.

Just like when we meet somebody we don't know, we ask for ID – it's the exact same when working with Spirit. You may only get a feeling, but nine times out of ten they will show you something that resonates. Or, before you know it, you'll say something that doesn't make sense to you, but it does for someone else.

Because it's all about you trusting yourself, it's about being congruent with what you say and do, and that involves a whole load of clearing out to find yourself in the first place. Maybe you just got lost along the way in between all the clutter that you came here with.

Work to clear and balance your crown chakra. Learn to trust yourself and your gifts.

In hindsight, the clairs all work together, it's not just isolated to just one gift. But in teaching ourselves to harness these gifts – that are genetically encoded into every one of us – individually, we break them down to focus on them, one at a time.

As mentioned, our claircognizance is blocked by fear, and we all have our own fears to work through as we go about our daily life. We're afraid the information we are receiving is wrong, so we second guess ourselves and can easily get confused with our own thoughts.

Happens all the time and stops me. I am continually working on this. I am a work in progress.

It's about paying attention, it's very subtle and very powerful when you trust it and use it. When you are open with a clear crown chakra, you ARE connecting to Spirit.

Through practice there are a few different ways for you to separate your thoughts from messages coming in.

Everything takes practice.

Thoughts develop over a couple of seconds and minutes when you meet someone: you might take in an idea about them, form your own opinion about their presence, appearance, their words, their energy.

It's a difficult concept to communicate – it's just this instantaneous knowing, an inner knowing. You can't quite put your finger on it, it's just there.

You need to be grounded at all times, a spiritual daily practice of grounding, anchoring yourself into being present and being clear minded.

Having positive energy gives us positive thoughts.

Negative information creates scary thoughts, too, so it's important to do some chakra balancing and clearing exercises using visualisation. It is a good daily routine to have. This will help raise your energy.

Our third eye and crown chakra are closely linked to your future self. These two higher chakras really do work together, helping you to find harmony and balance within yourself, which in turn helps you connect to the cosmic union of all that is – understanding that we are all connected. This can bring you clarity and the understanding that you are part of something much bigger, which offers you a space to hold all the knowledge, wisdom and insight into your life's purpose.

Working with these chakras helps us find answers through enlightenment, and growth through experiences.

The clairvoyant within you will peak as you develop your intuitive skills. You will automatically rise within into this "knowing", which connects and opens you up to your claircognanze. It completes a full circle of healing for you, offering you an understanding that resonates, makes sense, connects the dots and feels right.

Signs You May be Claircognizant

- There is no real standard of understanding if you are claircognizant, because it depends on your life story and experiences. Your story is constantly unfolding and how you understand life to be may change with different experiences. It is how you see and feel everyone and everything around you; your awareness of understanding energy in true form.

- Claircognizance is a deep sense of knowing – therefore, it is inexplicable how you "know". If you have this gift, there is a resonance of understanding an experience without having the full facts or truth about it.

- In all these exercises, we are crossing energetic boundaries that can only be felt, not seen. Your gut will link you up to experiences of what feels right and wrong. What you see may not be what it seems. So, trusting yourself as you progress will lead you to understanding people.

- Random thoughts or feelings will interrupt your thought patterns, and will be completely unconnected to what you are doing. When this happens, there is definitely some meaning in those thoughts for you.

Affirmations to Increase Your Claircognizance

- I am connected to the wisdom of the Universe.
- I am wise, intuitive and connected to my inner guidance.
- Every situation is an opportunity for growth.
- My imagination is vivid and powerful.

Work with your chakras to balance and heal yourself, do the exercises you feel drawn to, to enhance and increase the gifts you undoubtedly possess. It takes time, but is always worthwhile.

I know it's not easy, I have had a lifetime of experiences that I worked my way through. I invited healing into my life and my world has been turned upside down and inside out whilst I did it. But I always knew deep within that my flame would never be put out, and that little voice within told me never to give up. I believed I could do it and I never gave up on her.

I know where she's come from, where she's been, where she is and where she is going.

I will choose all parts of me that connect me to my past, present and future self. Three strands of my life, laced together in one beautiful braid of understanding, which were always intended to lead me back to a space of remembrance of who I once was before I got caught up in the deceit and betrayals that come when we seek validation from others.

I learned: if you need validation, seek it within yourself. If you want love, start with yourself; love yourself.

Anyone who offers me love, kindness and appreciation now is a bonus that I accept with a full heart.

Always Expect the Unexpected

Things never go completely to plan, that's the beauty of life. Accept this. Fear grips us from every angle when we face the unknown, when everything we thought solid slips through our fingers. Allow life to gently take you into your tomorrow. Have faith and trust in being present right now. What's done and said is over. Let the past remain in the past and accept that it brought you lessons in love and life.

My inner compass of knowing what feels right and what feels

completely wrong has well and truly been tested to withstand all the adversities that came into my life, but I had to do the work to realise what was mine and what wasn't.

Doing the right thing or being ethical sometimes isn't always the answer. We each have our own journey.

Who doesn't want happiness? Everybody seeks happiness within the silence of their own thoughts. If you are miserably unhappy, chained to what you think your life "ought" to look like for others to approve of, look into it – the only person you are letting down is yourself.

Being happy is an inside job. However, we do all tend to seek validation of it outside of ourselves, no matter how much we work to balance our chakras. It's our human conditioning to connect with others and feel loved and safe through other people and things that bring us the giggles, laughter, joy and happiness. These are of course important ingredients that we all need, but self-love and having self-compassion reaches us on a completely different level of awareness. It's you coming from a much higher place of devotion, it's you choosing to seek validation and love from that place deep within self.

Nobody knows your story better than you. The only person who can connect you to your higher, future self is you. Anything or anybody outside of you can't fully go there.

We can all feel the superficial effects of contentment in life; maybe that's all you've ever known. But when you find yourself on the other side of an experience that causes a paradigm shift in your life, that was a destination the Universe offered you, because that's where you were vibrationally at that time in your life.

This is when an awakening occurs. The lens you see through becomes clearer because you have made the decision to navigate through the fog of your feelings.

Notions and insights may have crossed your mind occasionally throughout your life. You may or may not have acted on them; that's okay – conditioning plays a huge role in our actions and you weren't ready to see and feel certain things at that time. You carry your soul experiences your entire lifetime, so when you're ready, they will come.

This is why "homework" for our "soulwork" is important. Soulwork allows you to connect with your soul's contract, and understanding it, which points you towards your purpose. This is the Earth School where we learn along the way.

My Healing Journey

I feel I have been chosen to do this work in order to help others through the pain and suffering that come with life. Maybe I have walked in your shoes and can offer you some insight, assisting you to find the strength to tap into the greatest part of you, the unseen layers that hold your greatest innate gifts that cosmically connect you to all that stardust you are within your past, present and future self.

Understanding is an art, not everybody is an artist! Creativity within oneself offers you the opportunity to create the masterpiece that you are.

Practise mindfulness with who you are at any time. Remember we are all moving, growing and changing, so all attachments you hold are also changing. This can invoke feelings within you for change, too. If your mind is constantly telling you that you're stuck and cannot change then naturally you will have a sense of feeling trapped and lost. But you can change things.

Have you a mouth that produces sound, giving you a voice? Your voice is a gift. Use it.

Have you ears that allow you to take in sound? That is the gift of listening.

Have you two eyes that allow you to take in the beauty of everything and everyone? That is the gift of sight.

Have you a nose that allows you to smell fragrances? That is the gift of smell.

Have you hands that allow you to touch things? That is the gift of touch.

Many people may not have all those things, but they will have their own gifts. If you are lucky enough to have any or all of these gifts, you came here to explore and enhance your life through contact with each other, allowing you to communicate and acknowledge each other's strengths and abilities. Every one of us holds our own innate special gifts.

These gifts unlock our free will and strength to make choices about what we will face along life's pathways, roads, roundabouts and crossings. Not every journey will be easy. That's the beauty with life – we just don't know where every road will lead us.

You can uproot and go anywhere you choose. However, think about your situation – what action would be for the greater good? Are you prepared to do the work? Finding your own superpowers to connect to the divine within you? Turning all those negative impressions you hold within into something pretty amazing and wonderful? That's where the magic lies. Let life guide you. The Universe is working with you.

Changing Perspective
Harnessing your inner forces of desire and passion to deal with any goal will see you through the darkest of times. Focus and channel your physical abilities and strengthen your psychic awareness to the here and now with all the tools available to you (chakra balancing and healing; affirmations; meditation, visualisation). Because if you combine your gifts it strengthens your development and understanding further.

If you have decided to change the narrative within you, then your narrative towards people, places and things will also change. Therefore, others will change their narrative towards you, too. As your lens clears, changes and adapts, your perspective and story, which have been attached to you, will also change.

Your communication with your internal compass and Guides will be imperative during any phase of disconnection from the outside world. This is when you are doing deep emotional healing. A range of different emotions will visit you – they will come from outside of you, raising questions about what feels right and what feels wrong for you and your present circumstances.

Your self-protection will be very important to aid you moving through any difficult processes. When you are hurting from an emotionally charged experience, the people attached to this story that is yours will also be hurting – feeling that sense of loss and detachment. How they express that varies from person to person as we all have our own walls and boundaries and are careful whom we allow to access them.

Maybe in the past you didn't set boundaries with your words, thoughts and emotions, didn't know what they were or what you were capable of. But I can assure you when or if you decide to start doing the inner work, the power of your words, thoughts and emotions will become very apparent to you.

You may find yourself dissecting every relationship you've had, asking yourself those deep reflective questions. Comparing your core conditioning belief system with what fits into your here and now.

You have got to be strong-willed to keep going forward with your journey. After all, this is your story.

As you learn to trust yourself, you will become stronger and will be less likely to allow other people's thoughts and projections to have any lasting impression on you. The crossroads and turning points in your life point you towards your destiny. And you can help others along the way – observe and trust how you feel, because by finding your own truths you become strong within your own story.

We can very easily get caught up with others – but remember, that's their story – it's not necessarily yours! Maybe you thought you were part of it, perhaps you liked the sense of belonging it gave you. After all, who doesn't want to feel that? Nobody likes to have a sense of loneliness. However, as we grow older, we learn.

You were created from stardust! We move through the ranks and transitions of life and with each step forward, we gain momentum and learn from any hurtful experiences. We will fall, that is definitely part of the journey, and that's where we get taught the most valuable lessons. After any period of loss or grieving, or hurt or turmoil, take time out, let go of all the emotional and psychic scars, evaluate your experiences, awaken your gifts by healing energetic scars and wounds, and your strength and determination will find you once again. This, in turn, allows you to go forward and help others.

If you ever feel you have no way out, sit quietly and take stock. Trust yourself and your intuition. Your soul essence can find you once again through what drives and excites you.

Being Present

Impressions are like core memories that are built within us. On a subconscious level we soak up everything. Part of our own unique blueprint, these impressions – and our core beliefs –can evoke long-forgotten memories that are held within every one of us. Memories that take us back to where life seemed so much easier.

Being completely present with what you are facing is a skill. This is why it's good to learn to be present in all that you are, and in everything you do and say. We are conditioned to run away from ourselves and that can sabotage everything for us. But every thought can create a word that belongs to a sentience we are familiar with. This is part of the loop we are in. The mundane conversations that come with life are meant to teach us when something isn't right. The beauty is – we can change.

Find yourself on repeat? Change your thoughts. This opens up new channels within our minds, our vocabulary changes, creating new pathways for us to explore within our mind set. This works. Remember the old cliché "If you keep doing what you've always done, you'll keep getting what you always got"? One of the symptoms of a mind ill at ease with itself and the world is doing the same thing over and over again and expecting a different outcome. Change your behaviour and you will change the outcome.

Remember, too, the infamous "What's the story"? I don't know really. I'm just working my way through understanding what that story is for me. It's leading me somewhere, I can feel it and it feels good, so I'm going with that. The stories I attach on to for others are important to me now. They didn't use to be; I didn't give much time and energy towards them. I most probably just sat in the "assuming" territory of life but I'm coming to understand the differences and learning to navigate my way through my thoughts, feelings and behaviours. And that helps me understand others.

I know where I come from, where I have been and what I have learned along the way. I know who I am and what is important right now. I am entwined with a thread of motherhood which comes first and foremost in all that I do. My challenges, my trials and tribulations are counted and documented within the library of my mind. I have healed, resealed and bubble-wrapped myself into a knowing and understanding that sits and fits for me. This has ignited a belief system within me that my children have chosen me for a reason. I count them as blessings that have fallen upon me and teach them to never lose that spark, their flame, their light.

My wish is to offer hope and reasoning to them in their times of struggle and hardship. They are my driving force and my greatest teachers in this lifetime; a tower of strength built on resilience that I can only teach them.

I am also an artist who creates and manifests through my drawings, writings and teachings.

Do I believe I am being supported and protected by something greater outside of me?

Yes, I do, right now in this moment.

Do I believe I am that greater force that can protect and support somebody outside of me? Yes, I do, therefore I will keep doing what I am doing.

Until a day should come that I lose this wondrous gift, I will keep going.

This is where I feel strong in my own spirit and connected to my creative team that are working through me here writing these words.

So many of us are not fully here in our present – our thoughts are either reminiscing over past events or rushing us forward into future desired outcomes.

We all have desired outcomes and that is to get to the other side of any heightened emotional experiences as quickly as possible. However, through these experiences you are upgrading your self on a soul level, reaching new heights of thought, of spiritual insight and enlightenment that "there has to be more". Being present is you asking yourself how do I feel? What is it I can smell? Can I taste anything within this experience? What can I touch? What is it I can see?

Any psychic abilities can be developed through your level of awareness and perceptions of this world. We all have the gifts and hold the potential to increase their power beyond any limitations. Practise, patience and perseverance!

Part Two

My Journey to Self

Parts Two and Three of this book contain some examples of my everyday journalling, which I challenged myself to do during 2022. These are my thoughts on how we live our lives, the problems and challenges we face – and why – and how we can help ourselves navigate them   so we don't end up forever bruised and battered, wondering what it's all about. It's about you. And you can do this.

I will also share some spiritual concepts with you, because they can assist you with working through any major upheavals, which are bound to happen during a healing process.

If you choose to take the route of healing, you are choosing to change your life, to improve and upgrade yourself to live in your "now" moments, which will help you rebuild a better version of yourself. When we do different, we get different.

The more present you are with yourself and your healing, the more everybody will benefit. At the beginning, like anything that involves deep and lasting change, there will be uncomfortable and challenging times. Consider these as turning points for you to step into your self. Do it with grace and kindness and this will invite more peace and harmony into your life.

I consider myself to be highly attuned to the psychic ability of clairaudience. One of the skills this ability imparts is automatic writing. To enhance this skill of connection to my own guides, higher self and inner spirit, I challenged myself to share this gift. I've chosen to do that by sending a certain number of personal words out into the Universe through social media. Although I had been writing in journals for several years before this stage – this was the year I decided to open myself up even more.

I would have no agendas, no clue of what would come in through me; it wasn't planned. I made a commitment to myself to get up at the same time every morning, light my candle, light my incense, ground myself, feel connected and just start writing. It has become a sacred ritual I perform every single day. And every day I look forward to seeing what is created, through me, right in front of my eyes.

My perception and awareness shifted. When I was going through something myself, the words and sentences came easily – it just started to fall into place. It's how I manifested another form of communication with self into a layer of free expression whilst I did the internal work of healing. My healing was happening in real time as I wrote page after page. It made complete sense. My journalling and writing offer me concrete evidence that I am capable, driven and passionate about my personal goal of healing and passing down any knowledge and insight I have gained along the way.

Writing is my anchor where I am present with my self and my time, as it's only when we are present that we make progress with our self. I have also come to understand that we all feel very similar vibrations at the same time each year. We have a heightened awareness because we are already attuned to nature's rhythms of change and transformation through the natural cycle of the seasons.

As much as I absolutely loathe certain aspects of social media – it is the turning pages of time right now. I write my words and send them out to whoever may find and read them. Social media is like a quick fix, however; my intention and use for it is simple: for you, the reader, to take the time to pause for a few minutes and soak in how the words make you feel. Are you learning something new from my perspective? By which I mean are you learning something new from someone who is coming to you from a state of a constantly healing heart and mind?

Those are the people I am reaching out to. I wouldn't expect anybody to read every single day. I just want to reach the one person who wants, and is ready, to make changes in their life. After all, healing oneself is a very intimate process. I am just a healing guide offering you your own set of keys to help you unblock any energy centres where you believe you may be stuck.

I can help you release your potential for your own personal growth towards enlightenment, and can improve your knowledge about your own energy field. What you do after our weekends together is up to you. The more you put into your self the more you will get out of it. I applaud anybody brave enough to step forward into understanding. Once you are attuned to healing energy, whatever umbrella you choose to learn it under, it's only then the unfolding begins – a journey of change and transformation will bring a new chapter in your life story.

If you are reading this, you have been guided to me during a time in your life where I can assist you. I have some knowledge and understanding of what you feel. I work on a soul level of understanding, not on a surface level of pretence. I have seen many battles in my lifetime, I have burned many bridges in order to recreate my life without people I once loved dearly. Why? It's simple: for my own sanity, clarity and peace of mind.

I know myself better than anyone else does. If I feel interference or discomfort with self, I take a good look around at the energy I am surrounded by. You may appear to me completely different physically to how I sense you. Sensing you and what you bring into my life tells me much more than the eye can see. I understand now why you have been guided forward – I acknowledge the growth in our time together and I see you in me.

Choosing to Change

Darkness became familiar to me; I knew it too well. Fear seemed to greet me at every corner, through conversations I had and overheard. My mind would go into overdrive and my body went along with it, rattling on the inside. My questioning mind became deafened by negative thoughts. My answers brought even more confusion. This was all I had ever known – 'cause I had no comprehension of how to understand what was happening to and around me.

The only way I can describe it to you is that I simply lost my mind and my footing. I was ungrounded and totally had my head in the clouds, which I now understand was a brain fog.

Fear had become my companion as I searched for my own light. I fed that fear daily with my negative thought processes.

But I chose to change.

I always believed in a higher power that was outside of me, and I believed that power to be in nature. The whispers, the echoes, the guidance came in through me. They would come into me at times when I was completely lost, raging with anger and frustration, feeling the pull to go outdoors to move and walk. The whispers would meet me at my most vulnerable, with a serene quality of calmness that always took me to a place of comfort.

My healing journey with Reiki was completely different because I decided to see myself through the eyes of love. Through meditation I was able to invite some peace in – just for me – for one hour. I would place my hands on each of my energy centres – the chakras – and repeated loving affirmations into every single part of me through them.

The truth was, before I discovered Reiki I didn't like who I had become or where I had been. I hadn't given myself time to heal through any of life's major transitions. I'd jumped so many different timelines, like we all seem to do, looking for anything to fill the void, like going into different department stores to see what we like or want. However, I didn't know what I wanted – I just vibrated in limbo, in a state of unconsciously "doing".

I had so much internal bullshit, trying to please everybody to the point of losing my shit. As soon as I would say "yes, I can do this for you", on the inside I was screaming, nooooo, I'm not available any more, I'm sick of doing everything, or whatever it is you expect from me! I was tired, tired of being tested, tired of hearing myself on repeat, tired of being sick, tired of hurting myself, tired of the parties, tired of the falseness of it all, tired of the hangovers, tired of noise, tired of being busy getting nothing none, tired of organising other people's lives, tired of the walls caving in on me, tired of blaming people outside of me, tired of not putting myself first, tired of getting everybody else's needs met…you know what I mean.

At the time I felt what I was feeling was everybody else's fault. And I was pissed off, angry, resentful, disappointed, frustrated, carrying a range of low-vibrational energetic baggage that I desperately wanted to offload. The heaviness of all the drama that I created consumed me.

I was in the eye of the storm. My only way out was to *feel my way out*. I did that through sincere apologies (regardless if they were accepted or not) and letting go. This was mine. I took full responsibility and did the work I needed to do. Everything I dived into touched my soul. That felt right – so I kept doing more of it.

That does sound pretty bad and extreme, but it's my truth of what I felt at the time. I wasn't a total wet blanket with life, but that is what

I was feeling. It's like I'm writing about a completely different person here, because I was a different person to who I am right now – and before that, I was yet another different person faced with a different set of circumstances.

Our lives really hinge on those destiny points I've mentioned. Your greatest mistakes can turn everything upside down and inside out. I'm still me on the inside, but with many more layers of understanding. I just remember the feelings of my old self. Maybe I did choose to wing it – I always think that I somehow did. I look at videos of my girls when they were so much younger, and – as I'm sure we all do in life – I think, "Where did the time go?"

I found myself in behavioural patterns that kept me down for so long. I call these my "knee-jerk reactions": stupid things I would complain and whine about because they seemed so much bigger for me to handle than they were for anyone else. I never realised that these patterns were brought on from my own actions. The whole "everything happens for a reason", might as well have been stamped in bold across my forehead before it went in.

It finally came to my attention and I knew I had to go back in time through meditation to sieve out the old me that didn't serve me any good, and make some changes

That's when I flipped it around to self, studied Reiki and learned about chakras and energy fields and how to heal and balance my self. I transformed my life, moving into the light through my writings.

So, life doesn't scare me as much as it used to. My fears became smaller, my strength of will and resilience to adversities grew. I did, and continue to do, the inner work that brought me to a place of understanding – which gives me peace. This is an every-day progression; I am a Work in Progress.

My aim is to keep going, as I'm definitely not where I used to be. I am totally connected to feelings and pick these up more easily than before. I feel I'm intuitively guided from one moment to the next. I trust myself more and, to me, this matters greatly. Trusting your gut isn't easy when you've had years of not listening to it. It's as if you have to keep convincing yourself to trust – because your body remembers everything. Your gut says – you haven't listened to me for years, why bother starting now? But slowly, with work, you change.

This happens when your internal compass comes into alignment with your heart space and you start creating the life you always wanted to have, with the right people around you who will lift and inspire you to be and do better.

Regrets, I've Had a Few...

Do I have regrets? Yes. Did I make mistakes? Yes. The choices I made during my life were mine. Perhaps they weren't the best decisions – but I now realise they were always going to lead me here to this time and place in my life. It makes total sense why I felt such a strong urge to never give up on becoming a healing guide.

At the time it seemed an extremely odd choice, and I did challenge every aspect of it. But the path was always marked out for me, and the signs became more obvious and crystal clear the more open and receptive I became. It all seemed a very natural extension of me but, at the same time, I definitely felt I was at the bottom of a very steep mountain with a long climb ahead. I had free-fallen down it and found myself struggling to get up. I couldn't breathe, I was weak, I was isolated. I carried my kryptonite for some time. Anybody that claims to be perfect, living in this imperfect world, hats off to you. Well done, congratulations.

For those of you who seek answers to your questions, and want to take yourself forward, you have no other choice but to do just that: start moving forward. Begin the healing process by working with your chakras, balancing your life, body and spirit and enhance the sentient gifts you already possess.

You will come to realise through your meditations that the signs were there all along. It was always part of your journey to guide and help others. Your purpose will become clear. Responsibility will come with more challenges – your own Guides will definitely put you through the tests before you're ready to explore a little more. You will get messages along the way from your teachers, Guides and spirit beings and through them you'll know that what you are facing is part of the greater picture.

Spiritual Concepts

There was a reason for everything that happened in your life. There was something you needed to learn from the situation you found yourself in, and when you were ready to digest the understanding of it, only then were you ready to move on. Every experience you have will leave an energetic blueprint of change and transformation upon your self.

Did you actually "wing it" through life? The hustle and bustle of getting yourself from A to B that only you knew how to? Maybe so? A possibility? Because choice was always an option. If you feel "stuck" in behavioural patterns where you keep hitting walls over and over again, you eventually come to the realisation that those patterns are brought on by your own actions. You find yourself in a continuous loop, and feel the need to get away from it all.

It's not easy to walk away – from responsibilities or the weight of others' opinions towards the choices you need to make, to get yourself out of the hole you've found yourself in.

As a society we tend to blame every person we feel is responsible for the energetic, emotional scars we carry. But their job is merely to point you in the right direction. It's your job to ignite your own flame within, to make the changes you need to make and to choose to be different.

Choosing to be different, is you choosing yourself.

What if you flipped a switch and saw the potential for growth in those challenging circumstances? What if you could harness the knowledge gleaned from your own experiences and use it for the greater good – your own as well as others'? For all those who don't understand why they are facing the same challenges over and over again but with different scenery and a different set of people?

You could pass down your knowledge: how you worked yourself out of the confines of the societal system, and are living your life as best you can even though your experiences will always remain a part of you.

Doing this means re-educating yourself about what you already know, but looking at it from an energetic point of view. This changes everything. It teaches you to master yourself with your own new beliefs and principles that work for you. It allows you to move through your day with ease, having a deep sense of trust with self. It teaches you to open doorways within your heart space that may have closed over time due to not understanding the point of the pain, or the personal growth that could result from the experience.

Your strength of will and resilience will be challenged whilst taking your healing to master teacher level. Just remember: you are choosing to live your life through spiritual concepts and principles that will keep you grounded. They are a gentle reminder of the great responsibilities you hold for others to learn from you.

Love Over Fear

When we choose love over fear, this allows us to bypass the pain and suffering of an experience because we are not holding on to all the negative aspects of it. It's as simple as that. Our minds are trained to focus on the negative. It's your tiny steps forward with positive actions and love that can break that habit. Doing more of the things you love to do – and of course helping others along the way. We are all in this together

Changing the way in which you live does not mean negating your experiences. Your experience remains, but you are choosing not to feed the trauma of it.

Trauma comes with so much depth and is very subjective. What one person views as trauma may not even scratch the surface with the next person. All that matters is your own personal growth and journey through enlightenment – and how it unfolds for your understanding. A journey of enlightenment is literally you coming out of the darkness of not understanding and finding yourself through healing. You just being you – not being influenced by another to change your course. As if you are swimming one channel and your attention must remain focused on "Forward".

This comes organically through your system and into your being, as you progress on your healing journey. Then you are ready to see the whole picture – the one that involves others, their feelings, their pain, because that's what connects us all.

We all change throughout our lives – nothing remains the same, yet something deep inside us whispers that we still remain connected to the person we were. If we all knew what our future held, wouldn't it be such a dull and boring life to live?

Soulmates

Soulmate energies are kindred spirits that come here to share our lives with us. Human beings have a basic need for connection and do not want to be alone in this world. So, we have tonnes of soulmate energy surrounding us every single day of our lives – it's a bond that keeps us connected to others forever in time. A bond shared with a certain level of understanding. It could be passing strangers offering you that smile, or someone holding your hand in your hour of need – teaching you the real value of what it feels like to be kind and generous towards each other.

We have really strong ties that come in the form of family: parents, siblings, spouses and our children. These people are there as you come into this world, or may be by your side as you leave it. Some people just know their soulmate and no matter what happens, they pull each other through the turbulence of life. This energy is soft, loving, kind and strong. It can be felt enormously if you reach a level of human understanding. However, it takes a lot of your time, patience and perseverance to de-code yourself through healing and dedication to self to reach this state.

I have come to believe that Soulmate energy is here to teach you something from past life experiences. When the lesson has reached you, and has been learned, it leaves your life. The difficulty is that we fail to realise when the time is up on our human attachment, and the bond lingers – which only causes us more pain and difficultly in moving forward. The golden opportunities for learning and growing come from the departures and losses in our lives. But something new and meaningful will then come along.

It's human nature to want to do the right thing in our lives. We all seem to think we have made wrong choices, but there was never a wrong choice. All your choices were always meant to lead you to this moment in time. You have been granted space to work through what you have learned from your experiences. Now, your healing can take centre stage and help you move through the changes you face. When you hold to your truths in any situation, you gain clarity about what steps you need to take to move forward. Doing the right thing can seem difficult at first if you are not used to handling or controlling situations. Self-control is your only way through your healing. By becoming balanced, we level ourselves up and stand upright. Dust yourself off and go forth.

Twin Flame energy can be very difficult to hold, as it's one soul that has divided into two (just like we see in twins, even though they can be polar opposites). It's not for everybody – it's a love that can only reunite when they are ready. It really is a relationship of total transformation through each other – going through layer upon layer of change and helping each other to get through life harmoniously. Finding balance through each other, not through self. The clue is in the name "flame". Fire can change or destroy the earth's surface, causing total disaster. If you realise you are in a twin-flame relationship, ensure the flames are kept at ease and under control: work together to help each other through life's challenging situations, always through a deep sense of love and commitment.

This is not an easy connection – yet can seem so hard to let go of.

Signs and Universal Guidance
We are never alone. There is always somebody watching over us from the other side. Their job is simple, to reassure us every step of the way that we are going in the right direction.

They may step in and make themselves visible during points of destiny – turning points in our lives. They will step forward into your awareness in the form of Guides, earth angels, spirit animals or even loved ones that have crossed over. They may be unrecognisable to us, just like strangers. But you will feel the resonance that pulls you towards them. They are able to assist you through your transitions, helping you make the right decisions through clairaudient messages.

So, take extra care during these times to follow your gut responses, and listen carefully to the people around you at these times. When you send an SOS out to your Guides / the Universe – whatever or whoever that higher power is to you that you are summoning – have no doubt, they will answer your call. It may be through a phone call from a loved one where there is a bond; it could be through a TV programme you are watching, or a song on the radio – it will be delivered to you.

The more open you are to receive, and the more active your awareness, the more you will be able to recognise your answer and how it points you towards where you should be heading. Your internal guidance system will lead you to a strong intuitive knowing. It will be either a pull towards something or a push away from something. You will reach an understanding and knowing of what it is you are to do or say.

Time out alone in nature with your questions is a great way to connect to these answers more clearly. You're literally sending your questions out to the Universe – your signals will be stronger and clearer and will reach more helpers or Guides to bring you what you need.

Acceptance is you acknowledging and coming to terms with the reality of your situation. What you should recognise here is that although you may have agreed to move forward, you still may not be happy about it. This is completely normal. You will never keep everybody happy all the time. That would exhaust you, and would not do your health any favours.

Promises will be broken from time to time in your life, and your strength-of-will tested beyond your control. This may bring pain and vulnerability. Finding ways to accept those things through changing the way you perceive life and its challenges, can provide you with a freedom from having to fight your way through every uncomfortable moment. Opening your mind to new ideas and concepts helps bring you back into a space of equilibrium.

Gratitude will play a major factor in your acceptance – I know this will be tough. It's you allowing yourself to go beyond the pain and hurt to find the blessings within the situation. What you gain from this is a new perspective which readies you to return to kindness. Gratitude is definitely a positive emotion and offers you mental and physical health benefits.

Focusing on gratitude, paying attention to the small things that may have previously gone unnoticed, can bring you a sense of joy. Thanking somebody for the valuable lessons they brought upon you, will have rewards. Observing and acknowledging the beauty and wonder all around you, and what you have created and brought into form, was always part of your soul work.

A good ritual is to make a list or mental note of all you have to be grateful for in your present moments. It's a great habit to get into. Feelings of inspiration can cause feelings of gratitude and this transfers to your surroundings.

Gratitude and love hold the same frequency, so when we hold space for gratitude for everything and everyone around us – we are holding space for love within our self.

Faith and Time
Faith is having complete confidence and trust in something or someone outside of us: a strong belief in something, where there is no proof;

trusting everything will work out as we planned. We all come here with a plan, a soul contract to one another. As soon as we are born a veil is placed upon us and we forget. That is the journey. We have a cosmic map that helps us navigate our way through (this) life.

You will come to this realisation when you are ready and open to receive more. Faith is the substance of things we hope and dream for. Never stop dreaming and believing that you can achieve any goal you set yourself. When we believe, we achieve. Always have faith in yourself and others to make the right choices so this world is a better place to live in. If everybody took that small step for the greater good of others, the magnitude of the effect would ripple the vibration of kindness throughout our world. Faith is unseen, but is felt and held tightly within the threads that keep us together.

It connects us all to a higher power beyond self.

Time – we are only here for a limited time; the only time you have is right now. It's what you choose to do with your time that's important. Time feels like a loop, chained to us, rushing us to the next place, to get things done, to be somewhere – we are always on the clock with our energy and how or who we give it to.

You've heard the saying – "time is the illusion; the only real thing is now". Our future and past are the experiences we hold in the now! So, doing what you enjoy *right now* cannot be replaced: the time is happening, and then it's passing, and then…it has passed. And on its passing, a new moment of now arises for you. Suffering in your present moment prolongs any agony of loss and detachment you may be feeling. This is why it is better for us to let things "go". Let pain go, and move on.

Yes, we grieve our losses, they will stay with us for eternity – until the time comes for us to say our goodbyes and a new doorway opens to reunite us with a gathering of loved and cherished souls. When we reach life's finishing line, make sure you have no regrets with your decisions. They were all part of your journey here on earth. So, when you consider time – choose wisely who you share those moments of magic with. Choose the soulmates who make you smile and fill your heart with endless love. Those moments will stay with you forever.

Meditation is also a great way to ask for help – connecting yourself to source energy, which means taking the time to plug yourself into Mother Earth for some much-needed reflection. The more grounded you are, the clearer the advice will be.

You will find synchronicities – messages reaching you to confirm you are heading the right way. Recurring numbers will bring in their own messages and, of course, your dreams will become very vivid. All these will help you see your situation clearly and will indicate what you need to do or say to help move your situation forward. These spiritual awakenings will change the way you perceive the world, allowing you to view life through *feeling*. Feelings can tell you more than your eyes. Your internal compass will seldom steer you wrong.

So, listen to your inner guidance first, above all else. Soul work teaches us valuable knowledge.

Karma Rules

Karma states whatever you put out into the Universe, the Universe will for sure give back to you, no matter how small or big – it returns. There should be no question about this. We never know when karma will hit – but when it does, it will meet you in a tsunami of feelings. You will know when it returns and how it feels to be on the other side of an experience.

It could take some time to come back, even going into your next lifetime. Karma is not cruel. It is merely justice, and it's fair.

Examine your actions on a daily basis – reflect on them, consider if you made the right choices and were these for the higher good for all concerned. Sowing seeds of good intentions will reap a good harvest for you and your future generations. This is because karma doesn't just take account of bad behaviour, it also returns good to you, too. The whole conflict of human conditioning is good versus evil, positive versus negative, darkness versus light. We see and feel opposing forces at work all the time. But choosing love over fear will see you through most difficult transitions.

Service to the greater and higher good comes with great responsibility. How it fits into your life is up to you. Contributing to something beyond yourself keeps your life in check and allows you to form a foundation of support and kindness. If we all took it upon ourselves to help this world be a better place for all humanity, we would bring heaven right back down to earth, a heightened vibration of love and connection empowering us all to be seen, heard and felt.

Balance is the ultimate goal. But this is an imperfect world. There will always be a great divide between what we should be and what we are. So much of this world is built on a need for survival; having enough to meet our needs. The reality is – to be truly fulfilled is to become the servant of humanity. Greed can take you into an abyss of self-serving, rippling pain and hurt. Adhering to the mantra "Survival of the Fittest!" can cause more harm than good. But offering your time and service to those less fortunate than yourself, or helping others to get through dark times is you spreading hope. And we need hope to have faith.

This has a knock-on effect that will open your heart up to have even more faith in people making changes for better tomorrows. If you have gained knowledge about how to live in this world, that is a gift you've been given so you can share it with those who need it. This is you being of service, re-directing your focus to outside yourself.

Forgiveness is mammoth and runs deep. It has to start with self. When you forgive yourself, it expands through all time and space for you. It brings feelings of ease to your whole being. Whatever your situation, forgiveness will free you from the hurt and pain attached to it. Forgiveness has great health benefits – it is healing in its highest form. Forgiveness is a process leading us to understanding. We have all been hurt by the actions and words of another and are guilty of it ourselves. Forgiveness invites peace into the self. Start with self, invite healing in – the rest will follow.

Life is too short to hold grudges. Yes, to really forgive you will face challenging aspects of yourself which are connected to lower vibrational energies – this is part of the process. Accept this as you go through it. It's not easy. You need patience and perseverance.

When we learn what it feels like to truly forgive, this is when our light turns on.

The Power of Love

Love is an intense feeling of deep affection. There are all sorts of high vibrational feelings that encompass us when we love another. People "fall in love" every day – but there are different layers to love and these, too, run way beneath the surface of our lives. Surface-level love is the law of attraction: if we desire it, it comes forward – as simple as that.

Believe it or not, there is a familiar thread to your love. We see another part of us in this person we love. They bring out our feelings of desire, our primal instincts, and a sense of wanting. If you feel unseen and unloved you will feel the desire to be seen and loved.

There are times when the whole primal dance leaves us and we become "stagnant", comfortable within our settings. We lose part of ourselves along the way when our attention is distracted. Fragments of self all over the place.

Being "The Chosen One" for another person, being and doing absolutely everything for that one person can be a tall order. We can easily lose sight of what's really important. There will always be external distractions and interferences, depending on how easily influenced we are and what personality type we are.

The dance is what keeps us alive; feelings of desire never leave any of us. We all want and need to feel special and loved by another, someone with commitment, who gives you a sense of belonging. Our trust will come and go with people along the way, but when there is a true bond of true love, you will get through to the other side together.

Don't allow fear to hold you back, because this will keep you stuck, and the only person you are hurting is yourself. Love comes from a well of happiness, from a place deep within you.

If you want to put effort into rekindling old flames of desire, or love that's grown "stagnant", it's good to give yourself a gentle reminder of the source of where the love stemmed from in the beginning. That's a good place to start. We tend to forget the good times as life simply takes over. Rekindle the memories and remember why you loved this person in the first place.

Love definitely comes with extreme highs and lows. The longevity of your love, and whether it stands the test of time, depends on where your devotion lies and what time and energy you are prepared to put into it.

There are no real feelings of attachment or love when we can allow ourselves to easily fall in and out of that state. That is surface energy.

Not real love. Who you decide to fully and completely give yourself to, warts 'n' all, are the special ones. Those are the couples who help each other back into alignment. If it doesn't last – well, it simply was not meant to be. At least you can say you tried.

Time is a great healer. For love to return to your life, be patient with your self. Fulfil your own needs in times of pain and loss – that will get you through to the other side with more ease. Don't focus on the pain, focus on the gain of the experience and where it will take you. There is huge strength to be gained from any painful experience. Finding and seeing the beauty in it is the real test.

Love is an inside job – when you learn to love yourself fully and completely you become fierce with your choices. Nothing will stop Love from coming in and reaching you.

Everything starts and ends with you. Allow the unfolding of life to come your way, you've already written your story. Whoever becomes part of it was always meant to be part of it.

Walk in gratitude, send blessings to everyone along the way. Nobody knows what it takes to be you. Master yourself and the world is your oyster.

Wherever you are, little one, this is your time to shine!

Part Three

My Journalling

I have chosen the season of autumn as an example to share some of my journalling with you, so I cover September, October and November, from the 1st to the 31st of each month.

This is the season of surrender, and you will find this a familiar thread throughout. We are all shedding at this time and we are in this together. I do mention some planet placements along the way, if I feel that should be mentioned to help ease people into their day.

You will notice that some days I take your awareness into the date and the collective vibration that we are under on that date. This, in turn, gives you a sign of which chakras you should focus on. The main chakras are the seven that run along your spine. Although I've covered them in Part One, I will also break them down for you here. Notice the sacral, solar and heart chakra have four dates. These represent the emotional surges we may feel during these dates. They open us up to emotional responses.

The thing to be aware of with vibrational dates is that they always break down into single digits. So, for those of you who may be new to this: 1 would be a 1-vibrational day; but 11 would be a 2-vibrational day (1+1=2); and the 16th of a month would, for example, be a 7-vibrational day (6+1=7); the 29th would be a 2 vibrational day (2+9=11 = 1+1=2). And so on…It's easy when you know how!

Corresponding dates that relate to our chakras for an easier understanding

1. Root Chakra: 1st (foundational work)
2. Sacral Chakra: 2nd (11th / 20th / 29th)
3. Solar Plexus: 3rd (12th / 21st / 30th)
4. Heart Chakra: 4th (13th / 22nd / 31st)
5. Throat Chakra: 5th (14th / 23rd)
6. Third Eye Chakra: 6th (15th / 24th)
7. Crown Chakra: 7th (16th / 25th)
8. Soul Star Chakra: 8th / 17th / 26th
9. Surrender; Accept and let go: 9th / 18th / 27th
10. Change and transformation; New Beginnings; New chapters: 10th / 19th / 28th

1-Vibrational Days:
entwine us with the Root Chakra; foundational work

1st September, 2022

As this date has a 1 in it, it is an "1-vibrational day".

So, today we work on our foundations. Are you feeling safe, stable, secure and connected within yourself and your surroundings? This is a day that the Universe will send you gentle nudges to assist you in making little adjustments to your routine. Jazz it up a notch. Come out of your comfort zone and be a little bit unpredictable. Test yourself, go beyond the four walls of the labelled container you find yourself in today.

Do something extraordinary, be daring, step outside the societal lines, cross over to the other side of the road, get to the path of least resistance, where there are no battles, just you being brave, being you…Sounds easier said than done, right?

We all have a fear of being judged for doing something that somebody else won't be happy with. But there comes a time in your life where you realise you can't keep everybody happy. You can't be that one person who keeps it all together for everybody else.

Be the person who keeps yourself together. Be fiercely committed to finding out what works and doesn't work in life for you; what allows you to be happy.

If possible, get a bit of distance between you and any problems you may have. Give yourself space to breathe, to access what you've learned from whatever curveball life has thrown you. Adapt. Use your knowledge of the cycles and seasons of change to reach understanding: as one season ends, another begins.

Don't Judge. Be Kind. Be Happy. Be You.

Ann

1st November, 2022

Well, Hellloooo, November! Here's another 1-vibrational day, folks, and we are shedding and losing layers in the mists of sweet surrender. The bonfires signifying destruction that makes space for new energy to come in, transforming old hopes and wishes to new, improved, upgraded ones.

This morning I would like to talk about gratitude – such a simple gesture of kindness that is free, completely harmless and allows you to regain your balance with life. The balance is you getting up from any falls you may have along the way.

Are you ready to take on this day?

Step into it with the attitude of gratitude.

Welcome gratitude into your life. Even towards people who have brought difficulties into your life. This is not an easy station to hold, but your strength and determination will gain momentum, which will allow you more space to fill your cup with what you need from life to allow you to move on.

However, forgiveness always starts with self. If you need to let go, release with love. An uncomfortable conversation may be required. You may find this a difficult task and usually this can seem much bigger in your head. A walk and talk is good for the soul.

You can also do this through a "cut the chords meditation". The person or persons that you are letting go will feel this as it is energy. Don't be surprised if they contact you shortly after this sacred ritual.

During meditation, you allow yourself to revisit a time and place from past experiences where you felt heavy lower vibrational feelings. Recognise where you are right now whilst sending healing to past events in real time, holding your hands over the space in your body where you feel and know the tension is held. The discomfort will resurface and you can intentionally work on releasing all fear-based experiences that have been held hostage within you. You are coming from a space of self-love through healing.

When somebody shows you who they are, believe them the first time round. However, we are all guilty of having made bad choices. If you are intentionally hurting or using manipulation tactics to hold power or to use another person, this holds and leaves a negative imprint: the only person you are letting down is yourself. Besides, it's unfair. Through your meditations you will allow yourself some peace of mind. It was never about you – it was always about the experience and how it affected you. We all leave impressions with others through our thoughts and feelings and behaviour. When meeting new people, be protective about your space.

Listen. Form your own opinion about what feels right or wrong for you.

What's real is how this person makes you feel.

Part of your Guide's job is to send you messages in the form of signs that come to you. The signs are very subtle indeed. Usually when you take the time to notice or even to think back, it can hit you like a tonne of bricks.

Sometimes, fear may have got the better of you. The whole "I'm not good enough" comes to us all as it's engrained in our society and has been poured into our container.

Whatever your instant reaction is, is super important for you to sit with. That's where your nuggets are for your own growth and improvement.

We learn from our mistakes. If you didn't learn anything from a mistake and didn't make adjustments to your life to ensure it didn't happen again, be careful. Some will call that foolish. The Universe will merely send you the lesson again – and again. Until you learn, and adjust.

Be grateful for the good times, they can be harder to hold on to.

Karma is real, folks. Acknowledge the lesson. Get back up.

Ann ;)

1st December, 2022

Good morning! Oh, my goodness. December 1st – another 1-vibrational date.

The silly season has officially begun. As much as the hustle and bustle of life at this time of year will take over us, for some people it's not a fun time. I personally assumed everybody loved Christmas – everybody seemed so happy, spending time together. I suppose when we were younger we didn't think of all the background stress to Christmas. It just went under our radar!

But for some people it was a daunting task: making it just right for everybody, making sure everybody was happy, everybody getting on – even just for one bloody day of the year seemed an impossible task. The whole house lit up, trying to fill it back up with the same energy as last year.

The reality of how difficult it can become for some people hits us when we consider the hardships that can come with Christmas, too.

Again, since we're in the first of the month, our awareness goes into our foundations – our roots.

So today, take some time to do some work on grounding yourself. I feel that just upon hearing December has finally come around, we place extra stress on ourselves to get going, telling ourselves there is just no time to stop, so much to do.

When you repeatedly affirm "there are just not enough hours in the day", you won't ever have enough hours because you believe it to be true. So, stop saying that. Change your mindset.

Today, make time for you to be still in the mayhem of your mind. Whatever this month brings you, don't let it consume you totally.

Take your time. It's not about perfection, it's about connection.

You don't have to do everything; we all don't have red capes and a big S on our chests! You're not Superman or Superwoman, or Superperson…You are only human – this comes with losing your shit a little more often than usual. Whatever your best looks and feels like for you, keep doing that!

Don't place any expectations on others to do anything for you, because they are just as busy as you. Everybody has something going on, whether they choose to confide in you about it or not.

Personal battles are on the rise. December will bring in a torrent of emotions for everyone. Be vigilant.

Be aware of yourself and what December brings upon you. Ease yourself into it. If you are in a position to donate, give to those less fortunate.

This little robin is a messenger of love to you this morning!

Ann

2-Vibrational Days:
connect us to our Sacral Chakra; understanding through relationships

2nd November, 2022

Good morning! Captain's Log for this 2-Vibrational day.

As I just sat down, a song played in my mind. Do you remember these lyrics?

Here comes the rain again
Pouring on my head like a memory,
Falling on my head like a new emotion.
I want to talk in the open wind.

(Eurythmics, 3rd studio album *Touch*; RCA record label).

Is it raining with you? It's definitely raining outdoors here, but it may or may not be raining with you.

Today we are stepping into a very high-vibrational day – I kid you not.

The 2nd day of the 11th month, 2022: the 11 is also a 2-vibrational day (1+1=2) and I hope you've come to understand if you are taking the time to read these posts that 2s are very significant here on this earth plane.

Because when there is 2, we unite and learn greatly from one another, thus joining our forces, combining and harnessing our strengths, creating a vision and learning through every outcome.

Every day is a school day! Every action and word you form into a sentence creates your reality; you are bringing it together.

Suppose I told you that you had three wishes for one day only? Well, today is that day! Eclipse season is a very powerful time indeed – all the planets we need are aligned with the mysterious water signs. It is a time you can make magic. Your intuition lights up new channels within the mind and you can make some new moves towards the unknown.

Be wise with your wishes. On these kinds of dates, get your pen and paper and write down what your heart desires.

Now, the only catch is – your mind has to be on board with this. You can say what you want, but it is belief combined with feelings that are going to override your mindset.

Thinking you can't is only your thoughts creating a story telling you that you can't. Your feelings create everything. Where's your antenna pointing? It must be upwards, because that's where your north star is: above you, guiding your internal compass every step of the way.

Go deep within today and find the younger you, the one that wants to be part of these three wishes – the one that had no fear or doubts – because he / she didn't understand. She / he just went for it anyway. Take her / him with you!

Dive into your ocean – is it raining with you?

Ann ;)

2ⁿᵈ October, 2022

Captain's Log: it's ChoooseDay, 2ⁿᵈ October!

Make a Choice. Take a Chance.

Or your life will not Change.

Sounds good, right? Uuuuggghhhh!

It's so much easier to be and to stay the same, hoping everything will go back to the way it used to be…when things were so much easier to handle.

Where there was me, myself and I.

Once you go down rabbit holes into understanding your life through the eyes of energy, there is no returning. You can't un-see or un-feel energy.

You sense things from people you meet, places you go and things you are drawn to. This wasn't just a mishap – it happened for a reason.

There was a build-up of signs before certain events or meetings in your life, but you probably never noticed them, until that internal light went from off to on – and there was no going back.

This is when healing visits you.

This is when you can become attuned to a new way of Being. You realise that everything you did and said brought you to this moment, where you can find yourself once again amongst all the white noise of life.

Nothing remains the same. Your vibe may take a nose-dive into those roots of yours and you most probably will spend a lot of alone time dissecting yourself and every relationship and friendship you ever had.

This would be a good time to get out your pen and paper. Or to start writing into a page on your phone or computer – whatever you prefer. Start journalling about your life. Start at the very beginning, as far back as you can remember, and throw some meditation and healing in there for good measure. Writing about it will help you understand more.

Alone / quiet time is all you need, but we rush here and there, going from one thing to the next, wishing our lives away. We treat challenges like hurdles we have to get over as quickly as possible before going on to the next one. And so, a cycle begins. Before you know in, you're repeating the same thing again but with different faces.

We all slip into memory lane from time to time, allowing us to revisit the past and see the view from a different perspective. When this happens, make adjustments with yourself, nobody else.

A Soul Journey is a journey back into remembrance about your self: me, myself and I.

So…who are you anyway?

Go deep with that question. You might not like the answer you were searching for!

Ann

2nd September, 2022

Good morning, World, Captain's Log for this 2nd of September: waking up to darker mornings, needing to give yourself an extra push to get up and at it. Maybe lying there with your phone in your hand, seeing what's happening with the world.

Here's some insightful information to soak in…

Energetically, with a 2-vibrational day, you will be doing work with your sacral chakra energy centre. This is located just below your naval, and is connected to the element of water, which means this is where our emotions lie within our physical body.

This is a very sacred space that holds all memory. It's the holy grail, so to speak. If you get lower-back or lower-belly discomfort, this is the body's Achilles heel when it comes to an emotional breakdown – this is where the pain body takes the hit.

The sea is an amazing source to go to when you feel any discomfort anywhere – but do go with the intention of working with your sacral chakra. That is, of course, if you are feeling any discomfort anywhere. It will go back to the source within you, which is this chakra.

Your chakra system works as a whole. I like to break it down for you to understand your light energetic body system. Having awareness of your light aspect is paramount when you are doing any sort of self-realisation / healing work.

In ancient Egypt, they called these energy centres ka, which is your soul essence. They believed that you came here as 2: a soul and a physical body – just like twins. These forces intertwined, adapted and evolved over time.

Over time, the ideas around these energy centres became westernised, with different names and teachings of how to work with these channels.

My doorway into these teachings was Reiki.

I read once if you want to know more about a particular subject you're interested in, you teach it! And as uncomfortable as this made me – I did it, and I continue to do it. If you would like to know more about yourself and your body, I can enlighten you and kick-start you into the world of understanding energy.

That said, I will always be the student. I will always want to learn more and want to build my little business into the most educational source for you to learn more from, too.

Top of the morning to you!

Ann

3-Vibrational Days:
connect you to Solar Plexus work; finding yourself; true self

3rd November, 2022

Good morning! 3 IS the magic number. It's the number of creation and manifestation. It's the number that changes the dynamics and shifts the pendulum, for all different reasons.

Whatever you are aiming for or trying to do, it can deter you, lead you towards your greatness, or merely encourage you by supporting you – this is your choice.

Everybody is just trying to do their best – that's it. I actually don't think that anybody would not want to try to better themselves by understanding more about life.

However, it can be difficult trying to rewrite your own story and reset yourself back to the beginning, where life seemed so much easier. We would all love to stay in a happy place, but the clock keeps ticking and time will always keep moving us forward.

You can choose to be either the grenade that keeps going off or be present in your here and now as much as possible. Each breath you take represents the seconds and minutes of your biological clock, and our batteries don't last forever.

"Go to the naughty step!" or "Go to your room!" Take some time to reflect, and when you are ready, come and apologise to anyone whose feelings you have hurt. These are small examples we see in every-day disagreements with small or younger children. As adults, we have a better understanding and usually know when somebody has been treated unfairly or is feeling hurt. Even so, apologies can be difficult to make.

Remember this. As we get older, we can reflect back and realise what hurt – slight or deep – we may have inflicted on someone.

This is not an easy situation for anybody. Not everybody is prepared to give an apology or admit they were in the wrong. Everybody has their own personal energetic boundaries where there is zero access.

Stubbornness causes to us to feel stuck, arms folded – "I'm right, you're wrong" – toe-tapping mindless blame games that will keep you even more stuck.

In those situations, the only person you're hurting is yourself.

Remember, you were never in control.

The Universe always ran the show, placed you in situations and circumstances beyond your control so you would get uncomfortable enough to make the changes that were always meant to be part of your destiny.

Destiny Points are you Changing Direction.

Ann ;)

3ʳᵈ October, 2022

Good morning, World, on this 3-vibrational day – a day for growth, for sure, where we are enabled to bring it all together, as we are working from our solar plexus energy. This is the most powerful source within us, this is where our flame resides. Yes, we all have this. Our very own internal sunrise and sunset. Invoking change and transformation from a place of authenticity, where we let go of who we "should be" for others – you know, the labels that we place upon ourselves.

When I first heard this expression, I was kinda confused. The Ah-ha moment will reach you when you realise you are in one of these roles, having a "label": daughter, son, brother, sister, auntie, uncle, friend, colleague, mum, dad – and in between all of them…

…There is you.

You...trying to find your place in life, where you fit in, a sense of belonging.

Just doing your thing to get from one place to another, working a job you most probably dislike, rushing to get home away from the busyness of it, only to return home and find you want to get away from the heaviness and responsibility of that, too.

Relate?

The space from one place to the other is where you are alone with your thoughts, maybe in the car listening to somebody who is so happy and excited with their life that it pushes you even further into the abyss. You think it's just you – you can't do it.

Yes, you can! If I can do this, you sure as hell can, too. When we strip everything back to our deepest self, we are at our most vulnerable. And when we reach that space, we release a whole load of conditioning and "beliefs" that we picked up during our life.

These include what we are and are not allowed to do or say or feel; what feels "right" versus what feels "wrong"; using other people as yardsticks to see where we are in life. When you begin to resist all the labels – and the yardsticks – you are beginning to heal. But you need space to dissect your feelings.

It's not easy to take or to admit responsibility; we are hot wired to blame.

We live in an imperfect world, where none of us are perfect.

Your life experiences add depth to you; embrace these aspects of you.

Always work from a space of worthiness!

Ann ☺

12th September, 2022

Good morning, Everybody. Let's take a moment – just you and me – and let's talk this out. On this 3-vibrational day (1+2=3) let's take it all back to our self-awareness and what and who we are influenced by outside of us.

We've just had a very intense full moon weekend, don't ya think? Did you nose dive into the abyss of deep emotional feelings? Do you know why or how they resurfaced for you? Or did you just kinda notice they were there but you weren't sure what to do with them?

Can you pinpoint anything that was said or done to you that prompted your mind to take you into a space of remembrance?

Thoughts come first. They trigger your body into a response or overreaction and, before you know it, you are within a storm of conflicting energies. This is completely normal – I ask you to listen to your body and what it is asking from you.

Full moon energies hold very powerful influencing forces.

The moon looked like a huge torch shining down on us at the weekend – in all her beauty, like a beacon of hope lighting up our pathways.

She was magnificent.

We are all deeply connected to our lunar cycles. The intensity of this Pisces full moon did not go unnoticed – I would be pretty sure that the surgeries and A&E departments were full to the brim.

Whatever tools you have to help you get through this would have come in really handy. The moon reminds us to reflect, to ask ourselves those deep burning questions that I think we all come to at some stage in our life.

What changes need to be made in order for you to feel better within yourself? Baby steps work best, one day at a time.

We are also in a Mercury retrograde in air, which really magnifies this intensity of energy. When Mercury retrogrades, we feel like we are taking two steps back with everything instead of going forward – a trickery of the mind is in play with these cosmic forces.

Air signs in particular may struggle most during this time. Know you are not alone with this. Reach out if you need assistance. Make sure you are in a safe secure space where you can express, and be, yourself.

The intensity of the energy is passing through you. Allow it.

Ann ☺

12th October, 2022

Good morning, World, on this 12th October, another 3-vibrational day which brings me to solar plexus work: the fire in our belly where we walk a fine line of understanding self through Ego.

EGO is mammoth. When doing any work on self-development, it comes up a lot. I was listening to Wayne Dyer recently and he used a concept that just resonated with me, saying EGO stands for "Earth Guide Only" – isn't that cool?

Ego says who I am is separate from you and separate from my environment, therefore I am in competition with you. The competition includes how much I earn compared to you; if my stuff is worth more than yours; if I'm better-looking; how much money I might have etc.

What is mine being separate from what is yours means having a lower level of awareness of what belongs to me, compared to a mystical awareness, which is a knowing or belief that we are all Connected.

In each and every one of us there is another being: the sacred higher self, that doesn't care about how much you earn, doesn't care about who you may be "better" or "worse" than – it has no interest in any of that. It's the part of you that just wants peace.

Ego says, "NO! It's much more important for me to be right." But there is no need for the struggle of who's right and who's wrong. The ego part of you will introduce you to stress, anxiety and fear, all of which hold a lower vibrational energy.

All of us are in a relationship with each other. Allow the part of you which is light – the part that just wants peace – to take over.

Soulmate energy is a person that you can work with through love, ease and understanding. Reaching those compromises with each other to create harmony and balance throughout the relationship.

If someone can push your buttons and send you into a frenzy, they are your greatest teachers. They will teach you that you haven't mastered yourself and you haven't been able to choose peace and kindness.

Do you love me for who I am, rather than for what I can buy and give you? Things don't matter. You come with nothing but love and you leave with nothing but love. Love is the bridge that carries you from one lifetime to another.

I love you for who you are, not for what you have or can give me.

If you were gone, I would miss you, but I would always love you.

Ann

21st September, 2022

Goood morning, World! Captain's Log for this 21st September. Another 3-vibrational day, so this morning this would bring awareness back into our solar plexus chakra. This energy vortex represents your light, your joy, your happiness, your authenticity, your power – it's like the ignition button that switches you from off to on! An awakening begins from this space within!

This, people, is the space in which we all should be working from, because it is all about the now; being present. When doing chakra cleansing exercises or specific homework with this chakra you will be doing boundary work.

This is our very own personal sunrise and sunset. It is our glow, connected to the Yang energy of "doing". It sits between two very significant chakras connected to our emotional layers (Sacral and Heart) that just want to Be present with exploring our feelings.

You may feel you don't have time to be present with all your feelings, reactions and responses – it's a busy and chaotic world to keep up with – life's not working out as planned…a lot going on…Yadi yada…

But it's about deciding to give yourself some time-out and self-caring the feck out of yourself; not focusing on what is happening outside of you, but what's happening inside.

Solar Plexus is your light, the fire in your belly, your gut that drives you with enthusiasm towards your desires, passions and goals. What is it you want from life? The bottom line is that we all seek happiness and joy – who wouldn't want some of that? Yet, we feel a sense of…I can't, I'm not strong enough, good enough…or we have too much attachment to the needs of others.

Not one of us loses our light within; it always remains, even though we may forget about it now and then. We all have desire, passion and drive; this never leaves us. If you are in pain, the depth of your pain shows you the depth of the love and light that's there. When you ignite your inner flame and reveal the light, you will rediscover your strength, courage, drive and enthusiasm. You will reach your greatness, where happiness will find you. Work to balance your solar plexus chakra in order to achieve this.

OR

Maybe you decide to choose not to be bothered – but why? Why give up on yourself?

You're the only person responsible for yourself.

Don't fret about the people who may not like you becoming unavailable – upgrading takes patience and time!

Loading…

Ann ;)

21ˢᵗ October, 2022

Good morning, World, on this Friday 21ˢᵗ of October. We are reaching a climax with the tail end of Libran energy. I'm not sure if you read or follow my posts, but I always send in a reminder that the tail end of any energy can be a difficult time, especially if you were ignoring the signs or any intuitive hits you were receiving.

This was a significant weekend with huge cosmic shifts happening – even the flash-flooding and thunderstorms around us reminding us of our internal storms that we push through.

Things are about to get a little bit Scorpio-ey, which means our investigative minds will come into play within the Scorpio season – as will our imaginations. But ensure you put a positive ring to it all. Please don't allow events to overwhelm you and take you to the depths of despair. We are conditioned as a society to fear the worst, but there's more than enough fear out there to tap into so try to keep it at a safe distance.

Sadly, we have no immunity from fear; it exists. It can take you instantly and, before you know it, your anxiety is through the roof, you can't sleep, it boomerangs back and forth throughout your days and nights, and your worries take form right in front of your eyes...

Even writing this paragraph makes me feel fear rising within me.

So, we STOP! Close your eyes, take a few calming, deep, controlled breaths with your hand flat on your upper chest; connect to your heartbeat.

Open your eyes, come back into the room. Notice your surroundings. Ask yourself: what do I see? What do I smell? What do I hear? What do I taste? What can I touch?

What can I do with this? Where or how does this process of calmness begin?

It begins with you.

To find the beginning (the root cause) of fear, we must often go back to the beginning. Sometimes we have to rewind and revisit the root cause of a problem in order to move forward. Going back to the roots is a difficult starting point because our current analytical mind is full to the brim with opinions, notions, conditioning and beliefs.

What are your beliefs now? 'Cause you're not the same now as you used to be.

We are moving towards eclipse season – be mindful of your decisions, disclosures and endeavours.

Recognise the differences we all share with one another: we are all similar in shape and form but hold different experiences within our chakra systems. What may work for you may not work for another.

Forgive yourself for not knowing better and break the conditioning chain!

Ann ;)

4-Vibrational Days:
open us up to receive love. Heart Chakra work; surrender with compassion

4th November, 2022

Top of the morning to you! Captain's Log for this 4th November. On 4-vibrational days we will all be vibrating from our heart chakra space, which is great because this is a familiar thread woven into the same blanket that rests upon us all.

We have all felt it at some time in our life – where everything just dissipates and there is nothing but love. Times where there are deep emotional feelings towards another. That feeling of unconditional love, a sense of belonging, a sense of being held, protected and safe.

It often feels like having your very own guardian keeping watch over you, ensuring the best outcome in all you do. This is what it is like when you connect with you Spirit Guide – this is your own personal Guide that keeps you within a blanket of protection. That's there to remind you of all the goodness you can tap into.

You are the whole universe; the planets are simply dancing all around you, activating different aspects of you depending on where they are cosmically.

The constellations represent different houses that we all step into at different times of the year. They hold different memories of our story that can be reactivated or deactivated. Some houses that we step into hold significant memories, long forgotten, that may resurface for us to re-examine. They are always there within our mind on an unconscious level that we may have simply chosen to forget.

These houses upstairs in the heavens symbolically hold our strengths, hopes, dreams and wishes. They provide us with balance, harmony and ease. These are where the good guys are that whisper reminders of the good within us, evoking happy, light feelings where trust envelops us and we are present with life.

We also have houses that symbolically hold our fears, things that are hidden deep beneath the surface. Those houses have the bad guys inside that whisper negative narratives which put you off balance, bringing disharmony and difficult times.

They activate different aspects that are personal and unique to you. As soon as you begin to explore these, when you begin to heal, when the timing is right, everything aligns, the planets, your chakras...

Your heart explodes, the stardust of cosmic energy activates every part of your being. So, on 4-vibrational days, work with your heart chakra – meditate, chant, use affirmations – to bring balance to this chakra and your life.

Ann

4th October, 2022

Good morning, World! Captain's Log for this ChooooseDay morning, another 4-vibrational day. Today let's focus on the choices you're going to make, 'cause every day will bring its own challenges and the decisions you have to make on how to proceed through whatever curveball or challenge you are faced with.

You've got to take responsibility for the choices you make, especially when they concern others. We all reach those breaking points, where we feel a sense of being totally stuck with life and we can't seem to get ourselves out of the rut.

As a first step, consider reaching out – go speak to somebody you can trust or feel safe with, a third party who is not emotionally connected to you. They can widen your perspective.

Sometimes, the emotional charge of discussing a difficult situation with somebody you love can become too much. You may feel as if you are under a dark cloud of judgement, but you are not.

The only dark cloud you are under is your own. This cloud is giving you time to rest and digest where you are with life. But remember, this time of taking stock and making decisions is when magic can meet you. In the space of your vulnerability – when you feel your own pain and hurt – *you've got to feel to heal.*

We all remember times when we said things in the heat of the moment. Once you say them, they are out there. Regret weighs heavy, guilt is even heavier, so it's just something to think about today. Whatever challenges you face, think before you speak. Work with your heart chakra. Aim for balance.

Words stay with people and can cause division. When we say things in anger, frustration is always near – this is normal, so be aware of it.

You always have a choice but your choices will usually affect others, just as others' choices affect you. As much as you think you may be alone with your challenges – you are not. Your Guides are there to help you.

Whatever time you spend under this cloud is up to you, but it doesn't remain forever. The storm will pass, a rainbow will appear and everything will become a lot clearer.

Happy ChooooseDay. Choose Happiness every single time.

Ann

13th October, 2022

Good morning, World. Captain's Log for this Thursday the 13th of October!

We are all on a 4-vibrational day, which, as I've mentioned, is all about the heart of the matter. We are all on a collective wave trying to understand the whole concept of luuuuurve.

A small four-letter word we call love that has so much meaning and depth to it, eh? How deeply you fall into it, shows you how much depth there is to you. And when you are deeply entwined in it and have that special connection with someone, the harder it can be to comprehend. It can seem overwhelming trying to understand why it's so much easier to fall into feelings of connection with another, yet so much harder to disconnect from those feelings. The disconnect hurts.

It's why we are here. Part of our individual life path is to get our hands dirty with emotions and feel everything. The turbulence and change that a disconnection brings can have a huge and profound effect on us.

Some people definitely feel more than others. This is when we discover empathy. Empathy is a key that offers you the ability to understand and share the feelings of another. Not many people have the ability to feel what another is feeling. I suppose that's where studying psychology might help, where people are trained to recognise your pain and help you access parts of your psyche that may be long forgotten. In that way, you can learn to heal.

The word "trigger" is a buzz-word right now; I hear it a lot. When somebody "triggers" an emotion or surge of feeling within you, pause and ask yourself why your body has responded to that stimulus in that way. That person has given you a key for you to access yourself a little deeper, which leads to better understanding yourself.

Love organically becomes entwined in everything we do and say. It's like we are all woven together in this blanket of trust and safety which is familiar and releases endorphins of happiness in our brain, which, in turn, affects our mood. We may not think consciously about a fabric of togetherness – we are just there for one another. It's instinctive.

Love is not tangible, just like our thoughts – you cannot grab hold of either, yet they evoke emotions and feelings in all of us.

Love is energy.

It's what makes the world go round.

Love is a very powerful healing force.

Ann

13th September, 2022

Good morning! Happy Choooseday the 13th of September. This morning I would like to scratch the surface of the EGO and SUPER-EGO (yes capitals as they are HUGE ;).

When I first came across these words I wasn't exactly sure what they meant so I decided to ask friends and family what it meant to them. Every person I asked explained it differently, which was cool – I gained lots of perspective and depth in understanding what these psychological terms meant. Did a tonne of Googling with it also, kept what sat with me – hence led me to doing a tonne of journalling about it.

Then I had this matrix moment of FFFUUUUCCKKK!!!!

We are all born into our unique self, which gains a personality, which is referred to as our identity, which allows you to express yourself to others in a manner that is socially acceptable.

Freud, who was the founder of psychoanalysis, theorised that all human behaviour is influenced by our thoughts, urges and unconscious memories. He also hypothesised that each human psyche comprises three aspects: the id, the ego and the super-ego.

The id is the primitive, pleasure-seeking part of our mind (think aggression, survival, sex drive, pleasure). It is entirely unconscious. It is the id that makes your two-year-old bang his spoon on the table and scream for food (food = survival. It's instinctual / primitive.)

The super-ego is our moral conscience (our "higher", "better" self). It emerges around the age of five, when we begin to take on those dreaded "labels": the standards and ideals of the society we live in (for good or ill), and of our parents and peers. The super-ego internalises those labels and standards, and strives to maintain them. The super-ego contains our conscience.

The ego is the go-between. It mediates between the animalistic urges of the id and the higher consciousness of the super-ego. It's the one that has to deal with our reality. It functions in the conscious and unconscious mind – the ego is self-aware.

For example, the ego recognises (feels) the outrageous urges of the id (I don't want to go to work today. I want to have lots of sex with my good-looking neighbour instead – and I want to eat lots of chocolate!) The ego is also aware of the super-ego, which is saying, "We must go to work to earn money for our family; we'll be arrested if you do what you're thinking about doing to the neighbour; and if you don't stop eating chocolate, we'll be sick…"

The ego's job is to find a balance between the "primitive" and "higher" parts of us. The ego is the part of us that ensures we behave in a way that is acceptable to our society, keeps the super-ego happy (don't worry, we're going to work, and the neighbour is safe…☺) and keeps the id in check (okay, you can have a small bar of chocolate, but that's it!).

The ego is where we – in our "conscious" minds – live day by day. The ego is a good thing, and only becomes a bad thing when it is damaged, impaired or imbalanced (and the id and / or super-ego then try to take over). There are SO many reasons that can happen, thousands of books have been written on the subject.

The super-ego is one reason why many cultures "clash". What we feel is the correct way to behave – because that's how we were taught by our parents and peers and the laws of the land – may not match another culture's rules.

We are not born with an ego (according to Freud, only the primitive id is present from birth). The ego develops over time when, as a child, we learn to master our impulses, and learn what is and is not acceptable behaviour (no banging your cutlery on the table and screaming for food, for example). At least that's what happens when things go well.

It helps us to perceive danger, store knowledge and solve problems.

"Yes you can!", to "No you can't!", placed in a line from what's right and wrong – as we grow up our feelings come into play and here lie the differences and blurred lines with our chakras' impressions and imprints towards people in our life.

We then have two challenging, conflicting forces. We agree or disagree with parental and / or societal lines so we push the boundaries and test the waters, so to speak.

(Teenage turbulence, remember?!)

We learn and adapt to the behaviours the world (in our society) requires of us. This usually stays with us. Remember, you always have a choice of Yes, you can; or No, you can't.

We all have a competitor inside us, seeking to be the best, to get something right or to win. We all want to defeat our opponents; it's engrained in us. We all prefer to say, "Yes, I was right," rather than, "Ooops, I was wrong."

Reality check this morning: we all have an ego, but try to keep yours healthy. Maintain balance. Work with your chakras.

Find yourself within the balance of understanding!

Ann ;)

31ˢᵗ August, 2022

Good morning, World, on this 31ˢᵗ of August, another 4-vibrational day which places us all under the blanket of love and connects us to our heart chakra.

What a chakra to work with, eh? It goes deeper than the deep blue ocean. It carries all our heartbreaks, losses, sorrows, grief. It stores sadness and feelings of loss even when we've forgotten the reasons for them.

We might see, hear, smell, touch or taste something that evokes a memory within us. Our gut / heart sends a signal to our brain – we have a thought and, before we know it, we're back where we had the sad experience. Then, unless we consciously break from the memory, we can go into a loop of remembrance.

Our mind is designed to remember the negative experiences. When you revisit any experience, your body still "thinks" it's there. Your thoughts then have an advantage over you – and your mind takes control over how you are feeling.

This is why it's so important to ground your energy. Grounding your energy, is simple – it's you taking a few minutes to bring awareness into your breath, the bridge between the body and consciousness. You take yourself into present awareness by being still and calm with your thoughts. Take your shoes off, connect to the earth's energy.

This allows you to become present, which is the safest place for you to anchor those thoughts so you're not up in your head, being controlled by your emotions.

Our heart chakra also connects us to love, a high-vibrational frequency that always remains with each of us. Yes, our spirit can get trod on from time to time with negative experiences – but negative energy is only surface energy and you can work with your chakras to improve this, balance it, heal it.

I meet a lot of people who can't disengage themselves from a negative train-of-thought when one starts up inside their heads. It is heart-breaking, it makes me sad – because no matter what anybody says to them, or does for them, no one can assist them in breaking free from this cycle of pain, except themselves.

You are the person who decides when it's just too much for you to bear. Unless there is a significant psychological reason or illness, you are the only person who can control your thoughts. You just have to choose to do so.

When that happens, a switch from deep within you will go from Off to On and the Universe will play a huge role in helping you to get there when you decide to take control of your mind and not allow it to take you hostage.

Take today as a new beginning for you!

Ann

5-Vibrational Days:
invoke change and transformation through Throat Chakra work

5th September, 2022

Gooood morrrning, World, on this 5-vibrational day. Okay, this day can go either way. "Like all days" I hear you say! Nope, there is always a cosmic pattern that causes a shift to take place in each of us on 5-frequency days. A shift that comes from a place deep within us.

You are the sole controller of how this will play out for you, so today be mindful of your thoughts. When you catch yourself going back to a time where you felt pain or discomfort – remember, as I've mentioned above, your body will think you are still there.

As much as we may want to revisit a situation in our heads, to go over how we could have handled it differently or better – that starts up a "would've, could've, should've" mentality within us that is not going to change anything. The moment has passed. You have been offered a chance to learn from the experience: to take something from it that the Universe has gifted, offering you a new perspective, new insight, a heightened sense of knowing and understanding. The cycles of time will not change for us; we can only take the gift the Universe offers and learn from our experiences – good or bad.

Whatever choices you have made, and however these have affected you, rest in knowing that how you handled them was a lesson in itself.

One thing's for sure: we cannot change the past – it has left us. If a particular memory brings on a set of familiar feelings and emotions for you, your body may react to protect itself. Our minds and bodies take us through a range of different low-vibrational energies before we can release the past.

This is perfectly normal.

Everything is energy. And whatever experience challenged you beyond your limitations or seemed too much for you to handle – it's gone. You're not there any more. You are here, in this moment, reading these words that I hope reach a space in you that causes the shift within you to choose happiness and celebrate the fact that you have already travelled beyond any bad experiences you may have had.

Behind that pain and discomfort is a hidden key that opens a doorway that leads you towards your purpose!

Ann ;)

5th October, 2022

Good morning to you! Another 5-vibrational day, so another day when there will be a shift in the energy. Today, make space for yourself to just Be. Be where you are right here and now.

I can almost hear you saying – where else am I going to be, Ann??

Good question…and my answer to that is "in your head". I know you know what I'm talking about – 'cause the truth is we all spend a lot of our time in there, you know…alone with our thoughts.

Uuggghhh, you really don't want to spend too much time there!

I've been a long time alone with my thoughts, trying to sieve out what's mine and real for me as opposed to what's not mine. In a nutshell, folks, that's healing, because it allows us to revisit all those upheavals and changes that we've had along the way. All those experiences that didn't make sense at the time but we just mosey ourselves on through like nothing happened, getting to the other side. I like to call this the "flip side" of the experience.

Maybe you've suffered a period of complete darkness – a very negative experience – only to find yourself alone, left to those thoughts of yours that run deep. You know the ones: that you're not good enough, smart enough, yada yada yada…

Listen up.

Everyone has a negative narrative running in their "thinking" mind, making assumptions and having notions about one thing or another etc.

That can cause a lot of internal frustration – you know, those crazy moments of "Aaarrrggghhh, I just can't think!" Or, "I don't know what I'm supposed to do!" etc. We can all have so much stuff going on in our mind, it sometimes feels it doesn't even belong to us.

We just want peace. One way of bringing this kind of peace into your life is to give your time and energy to people you value. People you can turn to when the shit hits the fan; people who can offer you understanding, with zero judgement.

Because sometimes when you bring up something that somebody doesn't want to hear, they begin to see you through a different lens. You've got to learn to be okay with this. It can cause a rippling effect that comes with more judgement. We cannot escape this.

There will always be a judge and jury to every situation you find yourself in. The trick is to surround yourself with those you love and value, and who love and value you – whatever, wherever and whoever you are.

Ann ☺

14th October, 2022

Good morning! Captain's Log on this Friiiday morrrning. Yay, it's the weekend!

Today we face another 5-vibrational day. As we now know, 5-days are all about dealing with change and conflict and having the resilience to recover from any upheavals and changes of circumstances.

Dealing with change is an inevitable part of life. As much as we want everything and everyone to stay the same, the truth of the matter is: everything changes.

You may feel personally that you are the same individual you always were – the same on the inside. But your biology changes and regenerates itself every seven years, like different levels of consciousness that you go through – just like your chakras hold the blueprint of every experience that is uniquely yours. Nobody else has your experiences or feelings; they are yours to carry through your entire life.

Another word that keeps coming up when I do Reiki is trauma. I've just Googled this word now (Google being a bit like our worldly brain! – Where would we be without it?) It translates the word "trauma" as being a deeply distressing or disturbing experience: your body going into fight-or-flight mode, which for me would be root chakra work – your Home Base.

This is the chakra that is most affected when your whole sense of self collapses, your sense of safety, trust, stability, when you feel a lack of support – this is where our fear lives and is often the root cause of why it can seem so hard to make changes with our "self".

We are all built with the resilience to withstand the adversities of life.

Cycles of change, through seasons and transits, are a reminder that we are forever moving and changing. Consider today what changes you would like to see or be.

Remember: if you believe it, you can achieve it.

Every one of us holds fear of the unknown, yet our reality is happening right now – we cannot change or forget past experiences as much as we would like. Only you can hold the past hostage within you, or let it go and thus free yourself.

If you want to move forward and live a life that is yours, you've got to dig deep, make changes and fill your life with whatever lights you up, whatever keeps you in the now.

We all have different opinions.

Be open. Listen.

Don't judge.

Ann

14th November, 2022

Gooood morning, World! Happy Monday ☺ We rise together on this 14th of November, a 5-vibrational day. As we now know, 5s invite internal change for us all, so on this kind of morning I ask you to observe your thoughts and feelings around any trials and tribulations you may be suffering. As I've said before, it's so much easier for us to remember and focus on the negatives in life rather than the positives, so try to catch yourself when you feel yourself going onto a negative train of thought.

Visualise a red STOP sign in your mind, or a red traffic light. Place your hand on your upper chest and take a few conscious deep breaths, in through your nose and out your mouth through pursed lips. Follow the flow of air as it enters and exits your body. Be aware of where you are presently. Align your senses and ask yourself, what do I smell? What do I hear? What do I feel? What do I see?

I understand that you can't all do this in the middle of conversations when you feel like you're spiralling. If that happens, just excuse yourself. Whether to the bathroom, or outside, go somewhere you have space to reconnect with self. If you cannot get outside but can get to a bathroom, just run the tap, place your wrists under the cold water, and breathe. This helps with calming your body and gives you an instant feeling of being present. Focus on listening to the tap running – that can aid with a feeling of cleansing.

I understand feelings of being overwhelmed. This exercise works well in calming us.

We tend to not acknowledge the good times, they can seem harder to hold onto. Train yourself out of negative habits by acknowledging when things are good and light for you. Consciously acknowledge how you are feeling, smile and be grateful in the moment. If you're sharing the moment with someone, thank them.

Place your hand on your upper chest with a feeling and sense of gratitude. Get into a habit of doing this. Hugs are great, too, especially heart-to-heart hugs where you really get to send and feel the exchange.

Just for today…Set the intention to become an observer of your thoughts.

Today brings new gifts and insights for us all.

Ask the Universe for a good day.

Be Kind. Be loving. Be You.

Ann ;)

23rd September, 2022

Good morning to you! Here we are on this 5-vibrational day, the 23rd of September and we unpack ourselves as we start feeling our way round this energetic house of Libra.

The house of relationships! If you are an air sign (Libra represents the element of air) you should start feeling at home. You will settle into this day's energy with ease and familiarity. You probably would have found Virgo's energy / constellation very difficult, heavy and draining on you.

You're home now and you are in your element! You've heard the old saying "she's in her element!"– well, this is where it comes from!!

Romance is the theme here, when we step into Libran energy partnerships, contracts we have with one another, energetic cords and bindings. You may find that documents need signing, as being in this energy for the next month will highlight everything that is related to legal documents, courts, guidance or counsellors – a third party of common ground.

May I just throw in here that when Mercury is retrograde, it gives you the opportunity to re-think things, especially about signing any legal documents. Mercury retrograde started from 2nd October in 2022. If you are signing any legal papers when Mercury is retrograde, read the small print. Make sure you are in a good mindset, hold good intentions, and take your time. Think it all through and don't sign anything thoughtlessly.

If you can hold off, I would wait till Mercury goes direct. The length of time varies for Mercury retrogrades each year, so always check dates. However, it will always be in the same element throughout the whole year. For example, this year 2022, it takes place in all the air signs Gemini, Libra and Aquarius. With this I mind, if you are an air sign you may struggle with decision making. Next year, 2023, Mercury retrograde kick starts the new year in the earth sign of Capricorn, and it will take place again in the Taurus and Virgo energy, therefore all earth signs may have a difficult time with their decision making, thinking they are going in reverse rather than forward. It definitely does play tricks with the mind.

Libra is ruled by Venus, the planet of Luuurve, so bathe yourself in what you love to do. You will instinctively want to do this, having weekends or some timeout to yourself. A change of scenery will do you good, helping you to breathe and reset.

This pertains to any 5-vibrational day:

Earth signs (Taurus, Virgo and Capricorn): you may feel out in the cold about something. This 5-vibrational day is offering you space and time to evaluate and heal this wound.

Fire signs (Aries, Leo and Sagittarius): you may feel you just can't control a situation. You can't fix or do everything. Take a step back and trust how it unfolds organically.

Water signs (Cancer, Scorpio and Pisces): you may be feeling a little low right now, you're carrying a heavy load. You're on a wave of transformational energy – go with it.

Air signs (Gemini, Libra and Aquarius): let go of any argument or anger you're holding on to. Self-sabotage may visit today, tell it to feck off! You may be feeling some hostility about things but remember: when one door closes, a new one opens.

Happy Friday!

Ann ;)

6-Vibrational Days:
offer us light into higher learnings connected to
Third Eye Chakra work

6th October, 2022

Good morning, World, on this 6-vibrational day. I really do hope that you get something from these posts. I just feel compelled to write every single morning – it's a task I committed to for the whole of 2022 and I must say I love it. It flows. This is called automatic writing, my true form of expression – some people would find it easier than talking.

The only way I can describe it, is that the pen / keyboard becomes my microphone. Whatever is "there" comes out through my hands and onto the page – I suppose just like when performing healing or doing cards, the energy exits through this space. Cool, eh?

Okay, this morning let's discuss this word "karma".

Karma, in Hinduism and Buddhism, basically means the sum of a person's "actions" in this or a previous life. It refers to cause and effect, which is an important concept, because it suggests there are consequences to certain actions. It's when we hear "good things happen to good people". But also, bad things happen…

This can be one of life's conundrums.

Whatever steps you have taken in your life to bring you to where you are now are past events. Yesterday is gone; today is the gift; and tomorrow is your future.

It's only your present self that affects your future self.

Destiny plays a huge role; we are not in control of it.

I know this can be a difficult pill to swallow, and it would take a whole load of wasted energy trying to figure out "why" every single good or bad thing happened to certain people.

Disappointment is a heavy cloak. However long you wear it is up to you; but it has a silver lining and is stitched with growth. If you feel yourself growing disappointed that someone who doesn't deserve it has managed to get a "better" life than you – put that nonsense away. Your life, and your actions, are all you need concern yourself with.

The whole past life and reincarnation belief helps me personally with moving forward. It's not for everyone, or in everybody's belief system, but there are people out there who specialise in accessing you, in order to assist you with coming to some understanding of you and your current and past lives. There are energy healers that specialise in past life regression, the most famous one out there would be Delores Cannon. Her work is phenomenal, she has a series of books that would definitely raise an eyebrow or two. If it's something that would interest you, I would recommend you look into the incredible work she has done and the legacy she has left. Her family continue to do her work.

Our future is not set in stone, we all have the power to change the direction we feel life is taking us in. We can choose to change any self-destructive patterns we may have. Little adjustments work best, a slow process of letting go in order for you to move gracefully through life while learning to understand yourself.

Ann ☺

6th September, 2022

Good morning, World, Captain's Log for this ChooooooseDay the 6th of September, 2022!

Today vibration is connected to our third eye, with it being our sixth chakra. I suppose you've heard about people having a sixth sense? This is when we are tapping into a heightened sense of intuition. We all have intuition, that small still voice within that we are not often taught how to use – although Part One of *Hidden Senses* will give you a good idea of how to develop yours. It's there for sure. It's also the voice you don't want to hear sometimes – like the good cop (angel), bad cop (devil) conscience within you.

You need to work towards finding a balance where you silence the bad cop in your head that provokes a negative thought pattern, and allow the good cop to encourage you with whatever you're doing or planning or hoping for.

We work in silence to harness and transmute any bad thoughts that we may be harbouring (which is negative energy that you are sending to your situation. It grows and you're giving it legs) and turn them off, or change them to positive thoughts. Let's face it, we are all guilty of this kind of negativity at some point in our life. So, it's pretty important we learn about grounding our thoughts by becoming present in our body. Ever hear the saying "Don't let your thoughts run away with you"?

Good cop positivity lifts your vibration and heightens your awareness, offering you the opportunity to tap into your intuition. This in turn allows you to continue having positive, happy thoughts. You'll feel good, protected and shielded from anyone trying to dampen your spirits – or to put your light out, so to speak. So, basically choosing to do what feels right and being the best version of yourself.

Our third eye chakra aids us with tapping into the good we see in ourselves when we find ourselves in our hour of need. We all have those hours, eh?! When you take the time to just BE in silence and anchor yourself to being present, shutting off your senses from the world and going to a place deep within you, you are opening this energy centre. Then you can take yourself into a sacred space where you can visualise your Guides stepping forward to assist you with any questions you need answering. By doing this, you are giving your intuition a way to reach you. Listen for the guidance and trust what it is telling you.

Tap into your potential today!

Ann ;)

15ᵗʰ November, 2022

Good morning, World, Captain's Log for this 15ᵗʰ November. Love the 6s. Any multiplication of the energy of the 2s, raises our vibratory level upwards and beyond as we reach the space of protection and float together in a cosmic layer of violet energy. I'm happy we are here today as there is a lot going on with planetary placements, so I feel we are safe here, rising above any situation that might induce a sense of feeling stuck.

Remember, you are never stuck. You will always be in the right place at the right time. Sometimes we may find ourselves in places that make us really uncomfortable. But remember, undoing yourself from any unwanted attachments takes time and dedication towards your desired outcome. Your thoughts can be your greatest friend or biggest enemy. Our thoughts can motivate us and give us confidence. They can also hold all our doubts and fears (about ourselves and others). This is the biggest hurdle to get yourself over.

You may find yourself being guided onto a path of healing to give yourself permission to breathe. Just be with those thoughts and concentrate on what you are feeling in real time. Sieve out your negative emotions. Breathe. Come back into the now.

It's all about learning to become present and still, and being lovingly present with self as you pick up all your broken pieces, which are fragments of you left behind.

Balancing this energy enhances our connection to our third eye chakra – supreme violet light shining in here, allowing us to access each layer of self. Which is fantastic. Every day's a school day, so what's going to come into this day for you?

That is the question, no matter what year or month we are in! As your day is just about to unfold, it's always good to start with a few minutes of calm. Listen to soothing sounds or even spend a few minutes chakra balancing, where you feel each of your chakras opening, ready to soak in the energy of what today will bring. I know this can be difficult with all the pressures of modern life, dealing with family or young children etc, but when you can, take a few minutes to yourself to breathe deeply and start your day with a sense of calm.

When we break each day down into its numerical vibration, and allocate it to a chakra, this really does assist with what coloured thread we will be sewing our life with today.

A violet thread will be on hand today, offering you a day to enhance your intuitive skills.

Your Healing Guide.

Ann

15th September, 2022

Good morning, World! A New Day. A New Dawn. This is Captain's Log for this 15th of September, which makes this a 6-vibrational day, which brings our awareness into our third eye chakra for today.

The third eye chakra is an extremely significant chakra if you are doing any inner work, as visualisation is a key that awakens this energy: visualising that bigger picture, holding onto that dream. It is deeply connected to any inner wisdom and knowledge you have accumulated during your life span of experiences.

Spending time with this space and focusing your awareness on it allows you to clear and cleanse any negative thoughts you may be harbouring. Remember, we are hot-wired to remember the negative, so in doing any personal self-development work it's imperative that you allow yourself space, a whole load of space, and time to understand what belongs to you and what doesn't.

Yes, it can be a difficult process. But it allows you to find yourself along the way and trust where life is taking you.

Our third eye chakra brings us on a soul journey of remembrance. Not a lot of people are aware of its potential. It works closely with our crown chakra, allowing us to sieve out the rough from the smooth, the ups and downs, and the curveballs life has thrown at us. It allows us to shed light on our situations, behaviours and conditioning.

Everything is divinely guided as we work our way through the process. Even when there is resistance, it is a golden opportunity for growth and understanding.

Being present is a skill that should be practised daily – even just for a few minutes.

There is a lot of cosmic energy in reverse right now, which is from retrograde planets. We are highly influenced by these external forces.

Go easy with yourself. Listen to what your body is asking from you and if you need help, please reach out for it. Reaching out to another is a huge sign of strength. Ensure you have a good support system that you can turn to.

Third eye chakra is also connected to your intuition, so when doing any third eye chakra work, you are fine-tuning your intuitive skills.

Happy Thursday!

Ann

24th October, 2022

Good morning, World!!! Captain's Log for this MoonDay the 24th of October, another 6-vibrational day.

Can you feel it? Headachey? Out of sorts? Vivid Dreams? Sweaty nights? Sleepless nights? The veil is getting thin. This week will be full to the brim of notions and potions, with magical properties coming to mind. Your intuition will come into play even when you're least expecting it. You will be asking yourself some questions. Have a notepad handy, and write down what occurs to you, because these will come in just like raindrops right into your consciousness.

Life may throw you a few curveballs and you may get distracted or even forget things!

There is a significant eclipse in the Scorpion energy, so make sure you don't get pulled down into negative thoughts.

Go deep into your mystique, your aura of mystery, where you hold your beliefs of what works and doesn't work for you with your natural intuitive powers. That's where the golden nuggets are for each of us to reach understanding.

Everybody thinks that intuition is the same for everybody. It definitely is not. This is why we can help each other when we make magic by igniting each other's flames, evoking transformation for us all.

Personally, I feel we are all too often in the shadows. Staying in the shadows of self can seem so much easier than doing the work, the work that is sacred and belongs to us. Doing the work we need to do to become balanced can be lonely and isolating. You've got to be okay with this. It helps if you do whatever you can to keep yourself present whilst also doing the work.

Sometimes life gets so busy with others that our thoughts can become confused. Remember, what's real to you is how YOU feel.

Time out with self is important for you this week.

Make time to ask yourself, "What are you feeling?"

What is your body telling you?

Butterflies, gut feelings, don't just pop up out of nowhere. Trust them.

Your Healing Guide.

Ann ;)

7-Vibrational Days:
offer us growth through experiences connected to Crown Chakra work

7th November, 2022

Goood morning, World! Captain's Log for this 7th November, 2022. A significant 7-vibrational day for all of you interested in your personal spiritual belief system.

Today we honour Samhain, what I have come to understand is a very powerful day. Samhain, a long-forgotten cultural tradition that is deep rooted within our society. The veil drops today. This is a day where we honour those that walked before us. Today marks the beginning of the darker half of the year. As we step into the Scorpion season, we welcome the shedding, the surrender, the releases.

Today we honour all transitions from the Human Realm into the Spiritual Realm.

Prepare to make some sacrifices as we stocktake to survive our winter.

Today is the day where you honour your own belief system.

What have you come to understand? What have you learned?

I feel that if you take the time to read my posts, you have some seed of belief that there IS MORE to you and this world than meets the eye.

Honour the space all around you, for it is filled with goodness for you to tap into.

This is a 7-vibrational day, which is connected to our crown chakra, so today I ask you to take some time out to acknowledge this sacred space all around you, that holds your very essence.

The divine lies within you.

Whatever that higher power is for you within your own belief system, I call it The Universe, which blankets everything together all around us in the form of nature. The Universe is always working with you, meets you half way with what you are working towards and always tries to connect with you through signs that are everywhere for you to notice – if you pay attention.

Winter's coming…prepare yourself for stillness and deep reflection. Today, sit in gratitude for all you have, for everything you have come to understand about this world and where you fit in it. It offers you a sense of belonging.

Light a candle with the intention of love, knowing that your loved ones are near today.

Ann

7th September, 2022

Good morning, World! Captain's Log for this 7 vibrational day, a day where you may face some conflicting energy, where there is growth to be had.

I'm here to remind you to invite some grace into your day, allow it into all your experiences, even those you may find challenging or difficult. We all face difficulties from time to time and have days where despair can take hold. We can lose track of where we are and what we are doing.

When you feel that sense of loss, notice what your knee-jerk reaction is: what is your conditioning with what you are facing; how are you handling it?

First, take note of the feeling and name it. This morning we are evaluating "loss". What does this feel like to you? We all experience loss. How that feels like to you is unique, but how you react depends on your beliefs and conditioning.

Whatever loss you have experienced, there is another feeling (emotion) under this – what is it?

Sadness? Heartache? Grief? Despair? Feelings of abandonment? We have a wide range of emotions that can become overwhelming as they affect the core of us, maybe even reaching older wounds that lie dormant deep within us.

For me, the initial loss is the "big bang". That leads us onto a pathway that goes through layers of our existence. We are emotional beings that are here to feel our way through these layers to reach our own understanding so we can find growth as we navigate the experience.

When we go through these layers of loss, they come with very low-vibrational feelings. There's a chain reaction that invokes more low-vibrational energy, such as anger, resentment, envy, jealousy etc. Because we want to blame somebody outside of us for any injustice we may be feeling.

This is when healing finds its way to you 'cause sinking into these layers for too long will have a detrimental effect on your mind, body and spirit. You come to the realisation that the only person suffering is you. So, you have a choice in that moment to sink or swim.

Just keep swimming!

Take each day as it comes.

Never lose hope.

Hope is something we all have, it's that light that never goes out and keeps us going.

Ann ;)

16th September, 2022

Goood morning, World, on the 16th September, another 7-vibrational day, and it's Frrrriiiiday! It's been an uncomfortable week, to say the least. The full moon energy may have brought up a lot of emotional turbulence from within, all the way up to surface level for you to feel once again.

Mercury went into retrograde and this added a sting in the tail. The planet Mercury is viewed as a personal inner planet that we would most likely feel adverse effects from, such as we may feel our mind is playing tricks on us.

Also, we have Jupiter, Saturn, Uranus, Neptune, Chiron, Pluto…these are our greater outer planets which are viewed as impersonal, and they have also shifted into reverse this year. These planets don't have as much influence on our personal feelings but collectively, as a whole, their influence affects the earth's surface. When Mother Earth is off kilter, we feel this on some level, though I suppose it depends on how sensitive you are to its cycles and changes.

I feel that we may see some disasters across the world that would change the earth's surface whilst these cosmic forces go backwards.

The influence of these planets can bring a wave of intensity, either high or low, going up and down and can leave us all feeling not quite sure why we feel off balance.

There is a sense of something going on here, perhaps some important change that will have a major impact on us all. It will sweep through everybody. We all tap into this – that's what I feel when I see these planets' placements. Of course, the planets' placements change every year. This is just what I feel in 2022.

We are also travelling through the tail end energy of Virgo, so organically we will be closing energetic doors and saying our goodbyes – until we meet again.

The house of Virgo is all about the final harvests, what you decide to hold onto or to let go of.

Our bodies are prepping for autumn, where we will shed once again. The New Moon energy may make us feel we are on empty, so bathe in gratitude for what you have right now.

Now is all that matters.

It's nobody's job to make you happy; it's an inside job.

It is a bonus if somebody decides to make your life more fulfilling.

Peace!

Ann ;)

16th November, 2022

Good morning, World, Captain's Log for this 16th November: another 7-vibrational day. Here we reach new heights, opening ourselves up to our "knowings", as we bathe in crown chakra energy. This can be a confusing chakra to work with. It's where all our thoughts and new ideas simply drop into our consciousness. It's bringing them safety down each of the channels of all the lower chakras, holding onto them and making them real. They dropped into you for a reason, because "The Universe", "God", "Angels", "Saints", "Guides", "Spirits" – whatever the higher Hidden Forces are for your own belief system – work in you and through you on a daily basis.

When you bring these thoughts and ideas down through your earth energy, you can manifest it, bringing it into form with your very own magic blueprint.

Nobody can add to these creative ideas as you can – remember this.

You thinking outside the box, is actually you thinking beyond yourself – knowing and understanding you are just a channel, a vessel.

You can share your insights through your learnings and can pass on your unique talents.

In clearing channels and pouring light into the dark, grey areas of your life, you are opening yourself up to tap into your gifts. We each came here for a specific reason and we work through others to find out exactly what those gifts are. You may not see them – but others can.

Everybody that was, and is, attached to every role that you have been labelled with is part of your journey, too. You summoned this energy. How cool is that!

Not an easy idea for some people to accept.

You've got to stay humble and you've got to internalise your truths in order to understand what you have been given.

Healing comes in many forms for each of us. Whatever healing means for you, keep doing that. If you have to fall off the face of the Earth whilst doing it – that's also cool.

Focus on yourself and if that helps others along the way, you are stepping forward.

Baby Steps…

What you give to others, you are giving to yourself.

What is real to you is what you are feeling.

Ann ;)

25th October, 2022

Good morning, World, on this 25th of October.

This was a rare moment for our stargazers on this day in 2022: a partial solar eclipse happened above us, roughly between 10.45am and 11am – it basically cast a shadow upon the earth, though the light remained.

Our moon passed between our sun and the earth. The moon represents our feminine, allowing us an opportunity to grow as a collective and tap into our greatness, which is our intuitive capabilities. As the veil begins to lift, cosmic energy begins to enlighten and enhance our abilities for our Soul's Journey.

It's a 7-vibrational day, which is of course connected to our crown chakra. That's no coincidence either. It opens our minds up to new possibilities, allowing new information to reach us. If you are doing any spiritual practices during any eclipse season, you will reap rewards!

Whether you are a healer, tarot card reader, psychic, medium – whatever your practice is – focus your intention on connecting and receiving messages.

We all have destiny points within our human life span. They are turning points for you to connect to higher realms within your higher self, aiding you through processes you may not be able to comprehend. Sometimes life can send you into a spiral where you feel lost and confused, but there are actions you can take to help heal yourself, balance yourself, through chakra work.

Whatever happens to you in this life is, I believe, part of your soul contract, made long before you got here. Any life-changing experiences are lessons to further your development.

Destiny points are turning points for you to grow and to make some serious changes upon self. Always stand tall, be the change you want to see in others

Baby steps all the way; take one day at a time. If there is someone in your life who is not good for your mental health and confuses you even more – take a step back and focus on *you*. Notice how your body responds: do you feel reactive, defensive, sad? Why? That's another key to the door to your deeper feelings, through which you can access more wisdom.

Your brain may try to convince you you're making it up, or that you should do nothing. But your heart is 50,000 times more powerful. Let your heart guide you. That will lead to your personal soul journey.

Invoking change enhances your overall wellbeing for your own personal growth.

Help others along the way. Guide each other into understanding.

Ann

8-Vibrational Days:
offer comprehension through breaking free from any conditioning. Educate and align yourself to spiritual understanding and concepts through Crown Chakra work

8th September, 2022

Good morning, World, it's an 8-vibrational day – a day to be consciously aware of your spiritual growth and connection. This day is connected to your crown chakra.

The crown chakra is located at the top of your head. I visualise this as a halo when I'm attuning to people with Reiki energy. When you open yourself to this energy centre, you are beginning the unfolding, or a spiralling, dynamic where we unwind ourselves. It's like we need to go back in order to move forward; almost like finding yourself at spaghetti junction ;)

The spiritual field can definitely be a land of confusion, when we have no concept of these energies and their effects on us. The natural flow of cosmic and earth energy is working with us at all times; we are all channelling conduits for these energies.

Our chakra system is highly attuned to the Earth and Cosmic energy. The current of energy takes us with it.

It's like we swim along through different channels in life. The currents push and pull us, taking us through a wide range of emotions. We finally reach land and need to rest, lying in the heat of the sun, contemplating where we are with our life – and how we found ourselves here. These channels represent a flow of experiences that we were always meant to swim.

We come to our own conclusions. When you reflect on the external factors that brought you to where you are in life, you acknowledge your journey and reach that total understanding with your self. Nobody can take you there. This is the soul journey that I believe is a sacred contract.

Move through your day in trust and let go of the attachment you have to your desired outcome. BUT (big but) never lose the desire, willpower and strength you have to reach it. Swim your channels, stay protected – find your flow and let your creative juices take you towards your wishes fulfilled.

Ann ;)

8ᵗʰ November, 2022

Good morning, World! Captain's Log for this Tuesday the 8ᵗʰ of November, another 8-vibrational day.

I get a lot of messages from people who come across my page and ask, "What exactly is it that you do?" This morning I am going to answer this for you.

I am a Reiki Therapist, having qualified in 2020 at teacher level. This allows me to teach under the umbrella of spirituality. I also take separate courses that enhance healing qualities which help support my core beliefs.

What is Reiki?

Reiki is an ancient hands on / off healing technique. It is based on a set of principles and beliefs where I channel white light energy into the recipient – my client. This activates the natural healing process, and restores and enhances their overall well-being.

Reiki is Universal Life Force Energy.

How does it work?

Treatment involves balancing the client's system. This helps them to cope better with a wide range of health conditions, including stress, anxiety, depression, chronic pain, infertility.

I work with clients on restoring their balance on all levels. Working with their masculine and feminine aspects, blending and harmonising.

What does it feel like?

You will feel an overwhelming sense of peace as relaxation envelopes you. Your mind will feel calm and your physical body relaxes as it is surrounded in the energy of healing. You will be guided towards having a treatment to ease your thoughts.

You will experience just Being Present with self, switching off from external factors. You may have a tingling sensation, heat or cold energy or nothing at all – depending on how you sense the energy coming through. It's different for everybody, but definitely a deep relaxation is always felt.

Benefits

Reiki promotes balance and harmony from within. It clears away and dissolves energy blocks. It also enhances levels of self-care as it promotes a natural balance with the mind, body and spirit. It complements other healing modalities.

Clients who come for Reiki are usually well and want to maintain their feelings of stability and clarity. It aids with balancing and enhancing energy levels to manage the stress of daily life or when transitions are happening.

You may come to develop yourself spiritually and experience a greater sense of the meaning of life.

I teach people what I have come to understand about Reiki. It opens different doors for everybody. It's a basic introduction into understanding self as an energetic being.

That's what I do, that's what I teach and that's what I promote.

Ann

17th October, 2022

Good morning, World, on this MoonDay the 17th of October. We rise into another 8-vibrational day, which is like the infinity sign on its side resting just above our head, connecting us to our crown chakra. This symbol comes up on some tarot cards, which suggests to me that the person is an enlightened being. That they are in awareness and are connected to heavenly / cosmic / outer forces and know that there is more to this reality and they create their own magic solutions.

The crown chakra is a very significant chakra, where spirit connects to us. Did you know the word spirit derives from the words inspire / inspiration? When we work with this channel we are opening ourselves for cosmic energy to enter us. We are allowing the magic within to shift our awareness into healing ourselves on a soul level.

This is when our spirit drops those creative ideas into our consciousness for us to work with, which can help us make changes upon our self. This can lead us from being selfish to selfless.

Any inspirational thoughts have been dropped into you for a specific reason, as you are capable of making it happen. You may brush that off as a silly notion, but seriously consider why you had the thought in the first place!

Instead of saying "I deserve", or having a sense of entitlement about things – definitely my old self's mindset, that I will put my hand up to – reconsider your position. The egotistic mindset of "mine mine mine!" or "I want, I want, I want..." is a tough nut to crack. It's hard to change, especially if you came from a space of lack, of never having enough or feeling that you'll never be enough. Working with making that change to your self takes mental strength, agility and power. You have to put in the work. It takes a lot of perseverance to reach this understanding.

When we reach a whole new concept of "How can I serve?", rather than "What's in it for me?" this is the crown chakra's golden light opening us so we can reach our soul's calling – coming from a space of love in our heart's centre; for self, because everything starts and ends with you.

As you change, everything and everyone begins to change around you also.

The more you put into yourself, the more you will get out of it.

Your Healing Guide.

Ann ;)

17th November, 2022

Gooood morning, World. Today we reach the peak of the internal climb – the top of our very own Everest! What a journey, eh? Each day offers you a golden opportunity to tap into yourself a little more. Today we reach an eternal understanding: we are all vibing on an 8-day, just like the infinity symbol that rests right above us, offering us sheer strength, determination laced with compassion, and offerings from outside of us.

The doors will open and opportunities will come forward when we are on an 8-day. We have heightened perception today as we stand above the clouds of doubt, which create storms of fear.

You can see the passageways, the steps, the people, the rocks, the trees, that helped you along the way to get to where you are. Today is a day that we express gratitude for reaching our destination. We feel connected to everyone and everything. Spend a few minutes to send heartfelt thanks towards those who gave you permission to find yourself.

The 8s are like loop holes, caught and entwined together: there is no beginning, no end – it's continuous – that's where we live.

The journey you choose to walk is the one that leads you back to your true self.

That's the unfolding of self.

Remember, as I've already mentioned, I believe we all have soul contracts, not just with our selves, but with one another. That is soulmate energy. We are attached to different energies for a reason. There's a thread of familiarity that we are all part of, the tapestry that holds our embroidered canvas together, which is part of the most magnificent masterpiece we call life.

Without you we wouldn't have the lands, lush landscapes, the mountains, the peaks, the snowy tops, the waterfalls, the valleys, the rivers, the lakes, the sunshine, the fires, the birds, the bees, the flowers, the trees, the weeds – we wouldn't have any canvas to work with. You are the oxygen that we all need to breathe and to keep our canvas of life going.

You are part of the embroidery that creates the rainbows after each storm that visits us. Keep the rainbows of coloured threads alive.

Entwine, embrace, plant your seeds for tomorrow.

Enjoy the view from your very own Everest today.

Congratulations!

Ann ;)

26th October, 2022

Good morning, World, on this 8-vibrational day.

Today is going to be Supercalifragilisticexpialidocious – even though the sound of it is really quite atrocious….

Ahh, yeah – it's that kind of energy. A little bit wiry, to say the least.

A little bit early for this trippy song in my head – I'm just trying to flip the internal switch.

1. Because I don't wish to come across as too serious as it can get a little intense during Scorpio season; and

2. We have literally cosmically stepped into this house of mysteriousness, so we tend to do a deep-dive into wanting to understand a little bit more about everything. The broom's by the door…

I really suggest that if you want to find out more about anything – start with yourself. Focus your intention on what you love to do, what lights you up, what brings you happiness and a sense of fulfilment. Concentrate on that, because it may drive you insane looking for answers – and happiness – outside of yourself.

There is magic available on these 8-days. There are candles to burn, wishes to be made. Gatherings and bonfires will transmute energy, making room for the new.

You hold and are a vibratory frequency. This varies from day to day as you work with yourself through others. The more obstacles you face, the more difficult it can be for you to see the difference between your energy and the energy of those around you.

Some experiences can open up your sensitivity and you may feel you are tapping into others too much. How others make you feel when you're around them is something you should focus on if you are planning to make changes.

Better still, find out what it feels like to be in your own energy, with zero attachments. Just let go of everything outside of you. This can be difficult to do but meditation is a great tool. It helps you to feel like you again.

Tapping into yourself will be the best gift you can give yourself.

We tend to get lost in everybody else's stories.

Find yours.

The rest will follow.

Ann ;)

9-Vibrational Days:
offer us time to surrender and release what no longer serves us.
They help us stay true to who we are, allowing us to move forward
through our days with ease

9th September, 2022

Good morrrnnning, yay it's Friiiday!!! This morning's affirmation on a 9-vibrational day goes a little like this:

Everything will be okay.

Silently repeat this when you feel there's not enough time to do what you've gotta do. No need to rush it – but rushing is what we do, eh? We're always going from one thing to the next, rushing around like crazy on the merry-go-round of life. You can slow it all down to your pace and what works for you. Give yourself extra time to organise your morning before it starts. Start the night before, by leaving out what you need to step into or do first thing. Fill your own cup before any curveballs and challenges take hold of you.

Time keeping keeps us on track.

Focus on that space, that gap between the doings of your day and breathe.

Everything will be okay…

Why do we worry so much about other people's opinions?

This is your story, your life.

Somebody will always have something to say about what you are doing – you are not going to keep everybody happy. The mind can be a destructive instrument if you allow other people's opinions to get into yours and affect / infect you.

Let people be themselves. Don't judge. Who are you to judge another anyway? When you judge somebody or think you are in any way "better" than them, you need to do a reality check.

Let's face it, it may be your ego that doesn't want to accept the truth – this is really deep internal work where resistance and fear meet us.

Aaaarrgggghhhhh! The dreaded fear! Accept it is part of the human design.

Nobody escapes this lesson.

Nobody knows you better than you. No matter how much you try and explain your feelings to another, they won't feel them the way you do. People can come to an understanding with you. They may have felt something similar and so you feel understood and heard, and you will be placed under an umbrella of familiarity, but your feelings are still uniquely yours.

It's not easy to talk about how we feel, yet we feel everything. Journalling is a great tool for you to take out and look at whatever is taking up your headspace. This really works and leaves a gap for you to allow new possibilities in.

Reiki healing is another great tool that gifts you being Present.

Reiki will find you when you need finding; you've just got to be open enough to allow it in.

The universe has a plan for you.

Everything will be okay.

Ann ;)

9th November, 2022

Good morning – as we sit under this blanket of super-charged cosmic lunar energy, it is no coincidence that we are collectively vibrating on a 9-vibrational day.

Sweet Surrender will be the theme for this day.

Zero harnessing. Zero manifesting. Zero perusing. Nada. Zero expectations.

This energy is magical for sure. Be under no illusion that it's not doing anything for you. This energy is swirling around us, propelling us towards insight and decisions that will align us with our destiny.

The Moon represents what's hidden: secrets, illusions – everything bubbling up to the surface in order for you to release and shed what you have no control over.

Time to get real, be honest with yourself with some soul-searching questions: what particles of yourself have you outgrown, that may not be working for you any more?

It is completely normal to feel "off", somewhat disconnected under this energy. Part of the whole growing up / aging process is that we are changing all the time. Adapting to these changes can prove difficult at times. Often your "story" is all you know so you prefer to remain invested in it.

Our sun, earth and moon are aligned, our moon has passed the earth's shadow – thereby bringing forward shadow aspects within you. Let life happen. When we surrender, and let go of any outcomes, they organically unfold for us.

Sit with this today.

I suggest that you go within and do some journalling about what you need to surrender. Writing is a powerful exercise. It kinda double-barrels your intentions of release. Your worries are not just in your head, you have taken them from your head and written them out onto paper. This can clarify them for you, so you can begin to deal with them calmly.

The moon is our cosmic mother and she is blessing us with ancient insight. This will allow you to be more open towards the right opportunities that will show up.

Be open minded to let your heart feel this energy coming in.

Yes, it's a BIGGY.

The Sweet Surrender.

Ann ;)

18th October, 2022

Goood morning, World, on this 18th October, which makes this another 9-vibrational day.

A day the Universe meets you, offering you the golden opportunity of surrender. Sounds so easy, doesn't it?

"Let it go". Three simple small words, that kinda slide off everybody's tongue like they don't mean that much. "Moving on", when to you the whole surrender is a journey, a process that is unique to you.

What it means to you doesn't necessarily mean the same for the next person – this is where our differences lie, our dualities. This is where we need to find common ground and balance that holds us together as one.

Every one of us is facing our own internal battles. We are all very similar in nature, yet we each have our very own coping mechanisms, that allow us to live happier and more fulfilling lives.

From the moment we are born, we are searching, seeking guidance from one another, looking for what works for us. You will know what that is the minute you find it because it fits like a glove – going hand-in-hand with a core belief system that keeps you together in balance and harmony. You will feel it from a place deep within you that resonates on a frequency of understanding yourself and others on a soul level.

That feeling of completeness of Ahhhhhh…I've found you.

It was you seeking yourself all along.

Today on this 9-vibrational day we are all shedding. Shedding old beliefs and conditioning that don't work for us.

Today consider this: surrender isn't easy, nor is acceptance of whatever you are working through. But know this: anything is possible if you put your mind to it.

Your mind is your most valuable tool. It allows you to access your brilliance. Creating your reality, reinventing yourself after any hardship, isn't easy – but you are so worth it.

Life is the longest thing we will ever do, yet it feels as if we have the shortest time to live it!

Kindness is free.

Ann

27th October, 2022

Goood morning on this 27th Occcttooobberrr! There's a kind of eeeerieness coming in. Hold on to your hat, point must be upright, broom by your side, because a sense of a magic is coming upon us.

There is excitement in the air, there is manifestation energy all around us. The cosmic energy is low and falling from the heavens, so near we can simply breathe it in and channel its goodness into every cell, fibre, tissue, gland, the flesh, the blood, the bones – every part of us that is in human form. It's helping us to dust down our container, fix our crown – literally! Because when it's fixed it allows us to channel and harness this cosmic wonder. We will fly amongst the stars and soak it all in!

Such a great visual there!

Okay, a 9-vibrational day. As we've seen before, this is a day of clearing. The more you clear externally, the more room you make internally. This allows you to take some breathers, to see how you are feeling. These clearing days can help you with difficult times – they will organically leave you. The narrative will begin to shift when you least expect it and, before you know it, you will have created a new beginning – all because you are focusing your attention on making whatever you want to happen, happen.

However, to do this you don't give energy to what is outside of you – it's all within you. You're changing your self on a soul level here. That's the sacred work, with your inner compass activated. You may be surprised to know who wants you to do well with your endeavours, and who doesn't. So, keep your plans – and self-healing – close to your chest (so to speak). If you want to share things with anyone, make sure they have your best interests at heart or are vibrating at the same frequency.

Otherwise, Chinese whispers could sabotage your plans. Chinese whispers are real, folks! One word borrows another, misunderstandings are rife, the conversation nose dives into a crash and you're just trying to do your best with what you've got.

What you've got is more than enough to make it happen.

Breathe in that cosmic light force, it's stardust – it's just part of you coming together.

Just be open minded and take note of the signs.

It's the Universe's job to work with you, not against you.

Ann

10-Vibrational Days:
offer new beginnings. Try new things, make changes and bring yourself back into the loop for foundational work

10th October, 2022

Full moon energy in Aries. Wooooow, did you feel it? Can you remember if you had some vivid dreams over that weekend? Well, you may have some over any 1-vibrational days – take note, folks!

Our moon is our cosmic mother. Everything in the universe – the stars, planets, etc – operates at a frequency. The frequency emanated by a full moon affects the frequency of our minds, and that controls our behaviour, feelings, emotions and desires.

Our mind is a storehouse of impressions, memories and thoughts that we accumulate over our lifetime. We remember a lot, but the majority is filed away in the vast archive we call the subconscious. The subconscious is exactly what it says: it operates under the conscious mind. It deals with how we feel when we may have forgotten why we feel a certain way. You may react with anger or sadness to something or someone and not understand why. But your unconscious mind knows why.

There is also our autonomic nervous system, which includes things like our digestive system, which is not under our conscious control; and our automatic behaviour – things we do without thinking, such as driving. When we are familiar with our driving, we don't really think about what we're doing – our vehicle almost brings us to our destination!

But when we are learning something new, something that's an entirely new concept, and we are panicking to get it right, it can sometimes seem overwhelming.

It's a learning curve. Whatever the new thing is for you, you have to be consciously aware and focused on the task or on the new information, in order to take it in. When you are set in your old routine of doing what you're used to, it's so much easier to say "this is too hard" and give up before you even start. You've got to be mindful of what you want to gain more knowledge about, you've got to put your energy, time and effort into that.

Yes, life is busy for every one of us – it's chaos. Before you know it, your day is gone, whisked away by the usual routine. Make small changes: make small adjustments today that will create some change to your routine. Small changes can have big effects.

Today is a 1-vibrational day, which is the Universe offering you a new start, a new beginning. Do some root chakra work, because it's foundational. It starts with you!

Where your attention goes, your energy flows.

Every day a school day! What are you going to learn today?

Put your "L-plates" on!

Ann ;)

10th November, 2022

Good morning, World. Can you feel it? There are a lot of planets in play during an eclipse season. The lunar eclipse is really playing havoc because it's uprooting all those storylines within the mind – remember, your thoughts are running the show here.

The thoughts come first, then the feelings play catch-up.

This kind of 1-vibrational day may trigger reactions towards people and places. Letting go of attachments isn't easy, because you may feel like you're losing part of yourself along the way. In theory, you are; letting go isn't easy for any of us.

We all know what this feels like. Every one of us has experienced a separation, a loss or disconnection from a person or pet we feel or felt deeply connected to. From teenage first love, that you may have thought you would never get over, to friendships that outran their course; the he said / she said shite and all the drama that comes with that.

There will come many times in your life when things are said that can get lost in translation. Trying to explain or express your thoughts when you are emotionally hurt can prove difficult. Especially if you have grown up being told that what you have to say isn't important – this kind of behaviour is engrained in much of our culture. Gets me all worked up really! Just remember: what you think, and what you have to say, is always important. If someone tells you it isn't, then you need to reconsider that relationship. I'll say again: it all begins with you.

You may reach a stage in your life where you want to talk about certain feelings because you just want to understand the difference between what feels right and what feels wrong for you.

This can become a huge hurdle, because you just want it to be right for you, you don't want to step on anybody's toes. I hear this all the time.

From the moment we are born, we seek guidance from outside of us: from our parents, siblings, teachers, peers, coaches, doctors, trainers, therapists, psychologists, mentors etc.

What resonates, and feels right, stays and we hold on to it.

This is your life, your story.

These are your thoughts and feelings – don't sit on the fence. Ask the questions.

What's right for you doesn't necessarily mean it's right for the next person. That's okay.

Deeeep Diving.

Respect.

Ann

Double-Digit Days:
come with high vibrational teachings. The veil is thin and gateways
for opportunities open for you. Master teacher energy will always
step forward to meet you where you are

11th November, 2022

Good morning, World – Master Teacher vibrational energy today – double digits greet us with knowledge.

"Hey, you! You're doing a great job!" Please hear your voice in your head repeating those words nice and clearly, in a calm relaxing tone.

You're doing a great job! Just take a moment to acknowledge this. Just thought I would start this Friday morning off with that statement on the off-chance that nobody has told you, because you are doing a great job.

Nobody smells, tastes, sees, touches, hears, knows and understands like you do, that's why you're so unique with everything you do, say, are. There will only ever be one like you. Doesn't that make you feel nothing short of extraordinary?

Today is a very special day indeed – the 11/11/22 – eh, helllloooooooo…All ducks in a row. You do know how powerful it is when there is synchronicity with numbers, dates and times? I'm assuming now that if you are reading this that you have heard of the significance of 11/11: it's said that angels and loved-ones are near. Their calling card, whatever that is for you, will appear.

Today is that day for sure. Elevens offer us windows into what we feel, and the knowledge that somebody is near and watching over us.

Let's say you needed reassurance from someone that you have lost, to let you know they still remain. Today the reassurance shows up for you.

You have literally manifested it to you through your thoughts –

that's how it works. How cool is that? But are you open-minded enough to try it? The thought found you for a reason.

Every day brings us a new beat, a new song. We get up and tune into the beat of our drum – our heartbeat. Attuned to nature's rhythm – she is shedding at this time of year just as we are.

Let the winds of time and change release all that stagnant energy you may be harbouring – nature will simply take the tears from your eyes as you organically shed.

We are all different channels of sound that can play the most amazing music – some days we may be out of tune, but the drum will always beat and will always take us back into harmonious music, allowing us to moooovvvve through life.

Love is infinite.

It always Remains.

Ann

11ᵗʰ October, 2022

Good morning, World, on this high-vibrational day. Today you may be more attuned to the angelic realm, and may feel the presence of your spirit Guides (who I believe are people that have crossed over that are looking out for you). They will aid you on your path of destiny, assisting you through those difficult moments and crossroads that we all come to in life. They are part of your ancestral lineage and will leave signs for you as a gentle reminder that they are there walking beside you.

Just when you think you may be alone going through a difficult time, you are not.

They are guiding you and whispering what you should be focusing on. These are whispers of inspiration for you to find your creative juice through self, which will help lighten the burden of self-doubt that we all carry from time to time.

This is the illusion, folks. When you hear that Doubting Debbie within your mind starting a negative narrative with you, know that they are just thoughts. See them just like clouds in the sky that will pass by. Acknowledge the first thought, but let it pass through you. Take a deep conscious breath in and on the exhale let the thought go. Don't let it grab hold of you, as it can grow and weigh you down for your entire day.

I used to be really good at giving my thoughts power, to the point where I would feel taken hostage by them. Meditation helps with stilling the mind and focusing your self in moving forward. It's not for everybody, but we also have active meditation, which involves dancing, singing, doing laundry, cleaning your home etc.

It's not easy to live in trust, knowing the Universe has a plan for you and you are being guided by invisible Hidden Forces that silently work alongside you every moment of every day!

You will just have this "knowing". It is guidance offering you the gentle nudge you asked for.

Today is a gateway day on this 11th of the month. The Hidden Forces will gather near and will let their presence be known to you.

Ann ☺

22nd September, 2022

Good morning, World! So lovely to hear the rain fall on this significant day. For me the rain is clearing the energy (clearing the air), getting rid of any of the Earth's stagnant energy. I love it, it's good to go out in it, and it definitely helps with clearing your auric field. Dancing in it is even better – dare ya ;)

I'm now thinking of the song by Madonna – *Rain* – definitely going to play it after I finish here!

Okay, folks, today we step into the 22nd / 2022. Love the 2s. Double digits indicate a Master Teacher vibrational day! All these 2s amplify the energy! This is very significant for many reasons:

1. Two is associated with our 2nd sacral chakra. This will enhance your creative expression and healthy emotions. And your mojo will be seeking some intimacy and pleasure. The divine feminine will come to the surface, and the inner child will echo through you as your intuition will be heightened. You can only hear your inner voice in the quiet!

2. It's where we create life. Trying to conceive? This is a great date!

3. Today is the equinox. We step into Libran energy, which heightens our awareness, sending it outwards onto all our relationships; working in harmony and balance; understanding differences; becoming aware of our light and dark. There is an opportunity to bring our past and future into the present moment.

4. We step into a cardinal energy here, where there are lessons in love. Cardinal energy means we have to go through and be the experience to understand it fully.

5. 2 is amplified to 4 (2+2=4), which bring us into the heart chakra, too; this is what Libran energy works with. Look after your heart, only you know what it needs from you. It's us who are responsible for love, not the other person – good thoughts bring in good feelings ;)

6. Love is the theme for this month. Such a small word that carries so much depth and leverage.
7. Heart chakra work can be difficult as it governs forgiveness and surrender.
8. Libra also represents Justice – finding your balance – but the scales are never completely equal. Work together and when times get hard find each other in vulnerability.
9. Good things come in 2s.

Enjoy the rain! Have a great day – positive vibes only
Ann! ;)

FROM:

Child to Daughter, Sister, Auntie, Godmother, Neighbour, Friend, Colleague, Acquaintance, Lover, Daughter-in-law, Sister-in-law, Wife and Mother.

I have had amazing teachers and masters through these roles that have brought me the toughest of lessons, all soul mate and twin flame energies that allowed me to access my abilities and give myself permission to dive deeply into the abyss of understanding my life's story.

Without everyone connected to these roles, I would not have found my own unique path and gifts. I am eternally grateful for every person that has led me towards this pathway. Without you, there would be no thread trail to help me go back.

Be grateful for the good times, they can be harder to hold on to.

Learn from the tough times and trust that you will get through them. They will provide you with an abundance of growth.

Your most treasured moments are like nuggets of gold you pick up along the way!

TO:

Author, Teacher, Healing Mentor, Guide and Spiritual Enthusiast.

I am a 13th-generation Reiki Master Teacher for the lineage of Shiki Ryoho Usui, Dublin, Ireland.

I hold workshops for teaching Reiki Self-Healing Level 1, 2 and 3 alongside holding Reiki Shares.

I offer Psychic Development workshops and by the end of 2023 I plan to teach Tarot workshops. For those interested in attending these classes, keep an eye on my social media platforms. I'm on Instagram, Facebook and Linkedin as Ann Traynor Wellness Centre. I'm also the author of *Hidden Forces*, which is the perfect complement to *Hidden Senses*.

Google Ann Traynor and you'll find me on these platforms and how to connect with me.

Website is: anntraynorwellnesscentre.ie.

I am all that I am, Ann Traynor ;)

Printed in Great Britain
by Amazon

19373407R00112